# THE VINTAGE YEARS
## — OF —
# MOTORING

# THE VINTAGE YEARS
## —— OF ——
# MOTORING
## 1920s & 1930s

## A. B. DEMAUS

AMBERLEY

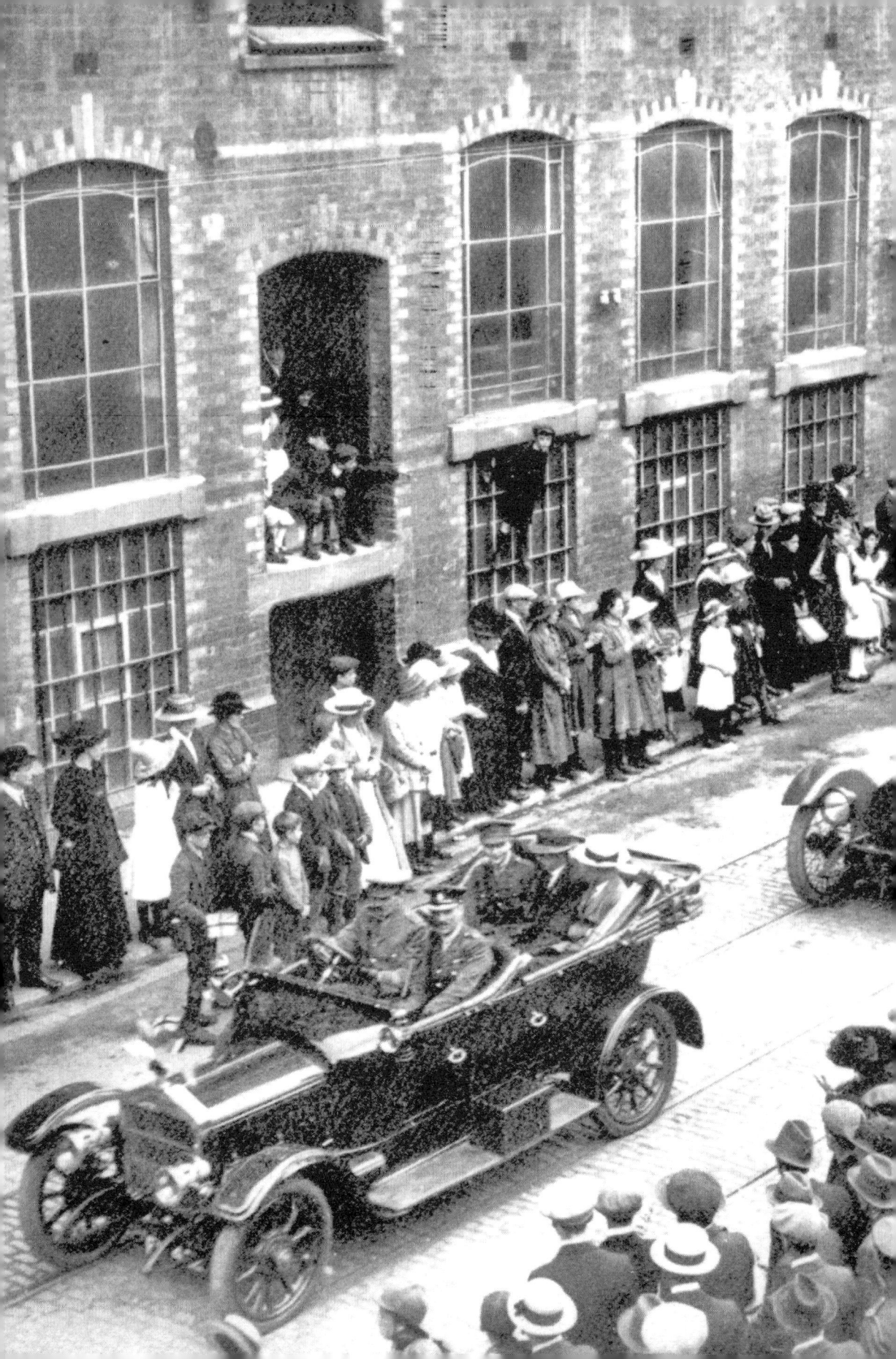

*Frontispiece:* The dawn of a new era. A formal armistice parade passes through the streets of Worcester in 1918 with a Singer, a Crossley, a Vauxhall 'Prince Henry' and a Daimler leading the procession. The cars all date from the pre-war period but the coming of peace did not restore the old order, which had gone forever. Although this parade marked the end of 'the war to end all wars', the majority of those present would be embroiled in war again after only twenty-one years. (*J. E. Stanford*)

First published 1979
This edition first published 2012

Amberley Publishing
The Hill, Stroud,
Gloucestershire, GL5 4EP

www.amberleybooks.com

Copyright © A. B. Demaus, 2012

The right of A. B. Demaus to be identified as the Author
of this work has been asserted in accordance with the
Copyrights, Designs and Patents Act 1988.

All rights reserved. No part of this book may be reprinted
or reproduced or utilised in any form or by any electronic,
mechanical or other means, now known or hereafter invented, including
photocopying and recording, or in any information
storage or retrieval system, without the permission in writing
from the Publishers.

British Library Cataloguing in Publication Data.
A catalogue record for this book is available from the British Library.

ISBN 978 1 84868 465 2

Typesetting and Origination by Amberley Publishing.
Printed in Great Britain.

# CONTENTS

|   | Acknowledgements | 8 |
|---|---|---|
|   | Introduction | 9 |
| 1 | Motorcycling | 11 |
| 2 | Cyclecars & Babies | 25 |
| 3 | Going for a Spin | 35 |
| 4 | Motoring... Almost for the Masses | 53 |
| 5 | Sport | 69 |
| 6 | Serving the Public | 89 |
| 7 | Repairs & Replenishments | 103 |
| 8 | Traffic & Accidents | 113 |
|   | About the Author | 125 |

# ACKNOWLEDGEMENTS

The author owes a real debt of gratitude to innumerable people who have endured, put up with, or even in any way encouraged his obsessive love of motorcars since the age of four or thereabouts, and in a narrower field but with no less genuine gratitude to the many who have most kindly allowed him access to private photographs of motoring topics. Because the majority of the photographs have come from private sources it has not always been possible to identify the photographer or the original source with any certainty, and if someone's copyright has thus been inadvertently infringed, the author craves forgiveness and indulgence.

# INTRODUCTION

Motorcars and motoring as a pastime had only been in existence for approximately two decades by the time the 1918 armistice was signed. In that short period technical advances had been prodigious, whereas in the following two decades, with which this book is concerned, the technical advances were far less immediately apparent; one had to look beneath the surface, so to speak, to find them. To express this in another way, the motorcar of 1938 was, in its capabilities and appearance, far less different from that of 1918 than was the motorcar of 1918 from that of 1898.

To regard motoring between the wars solely in the light of technical progress is to lose sight of what is perhaps the key factor in assessing the differences that distinguish the 1920s and '30s motoring scene from that prior to 1914. This key factor lies much more with the social and economic climate and environment, of which motoring in the inter-war years became an increasingly significant part, than in the technical progress of the cars themselves.

There was such progress, of course, for cars such as the Leyland Eight, the Lanchester Forty, the Isotta-Fraschini Tipo 8 or the Hispano-Suiza H6B and others were splendid evidence of it. These were costly machines, aiming for perfection in a market where cost was of little or no consequence. Had their designers been able to look forward to 1938 they might have seen, no doubt to their dismay, to what tiny proportions that market would by then have shrunk. Rather it was Henry Ford or William Morris whose vision was to be proved the sounder, for the one consistent theme for the following twenty years was the achievement of motoring for the masses; not in the cheap and crude cyclecars but in no-nonsense, go-anywhere, easy-to-maintain, inexpensive and unpretentious cars for which they rightly saw an ever-expanding market.

For the majority of motorists of, say, 1938, the car or motorcycle was merely a means of getting from A to B. True, it may have been used purely 'for pleasure' at weekends and in the holidays, but it was not used for motoring's sake, for the pleasures and sensations that motoring gave. Ten years earlier the majority of cars would have been used with the pleasure of motoring as an activity, a sensation, slightly uppermost, overruling the mere idea of getting from place to place; while in 1918, if one was lucky enough to own a motor vehicle at all, the pleasure of actually motoring, the sensation, was the prime incentive. Obviously these criteria apply only in general terms to that mythical being, 'the average motorist' – to the enthusiasts of any motoring period, as for the enthusiasts for any other pastimes, different values must be applied.

In selecting the photographs, the aim has been to show motoring between the wars in as wide a variety as possible, but, inevitably, much has had to be left out. Those who were motorists in this period, particularly in the earlier years of it, may well be disappointed that the make or model they best remember isn't portrayed, an omission that may be equally regretted by those whose interest in the subject stems from reasons other than of having motored in those seemingly far-off days. But no amount of photographs can be a total substitute for first-hand experience; if one has that experience, one adds one's own imagination to the picture to conjure up the thousand fleeting impressions of the time… one can hear the individual engine note, smell the leather upholstery, recall the squeaking brakes when one was on the way to so-and-so. If one lacks that experience then, sadly, it is rather like looking through an old album that belonged to strangers… one sees the pictures and can recognise objects, but the essence, the momentary reliving of times, places and sensations, is lacking and one can only wonder what it was really all about. To wonder is a valuable aid to one's sense of proportion and one doesn't need to know all the answers; to wonder is good enough.

A less formal Armistice celebration. Somebody put in hours of work (and robbed the bathroom floor of yards of covering!) to decorate this American car for the occasion. To these youngsters, drawn from nursing and the three services, belonged the next two decades. What would they make of them? (*National Library of Wales*)

# 1
# MOTORCYCLING

The years between the wars saw the zenith of the British motorcycle, but it was a period during which both the pastime itself and the machines underwent a number of subtle changes. Broadly speaking, the motorcycle appealed to the sportsman in that in sporting guise it offered a performance better than could be achieved in a car except at many times the initial cost and cost of running, whereas its appeal to the tourist was predominantly that of low initial cost and upkeep, with performance coming a long way behind in his priorities.

The one fly in the ointment was the lack of weather protection and the resultant need for specialised clothing to combat the elements. This was of little consequence to the rabid sporting enthusiast who was inclined to regard even the most spartan car owner as something of a sybarite, but it was of consequence to the 'potterer' or the family man.

The motorcycle had played a prominent part in the recent war, and many thousands of servicemen were familiar with the trusty Triumphs and flat-twin Douglases and other machines that had given such yeoman service. Peace brought few new designs at first, but the rush to become mobile created a rash of small makers, often mere assemblers, who turned out machines of little merit. Direct belt drive was on the way out, except in the lowest-powered and cheapest machines, but chain-cum-belt drive was still commonplace, as were machines lacking either a kick-starter or even a free-engine clutch. Some riders still preferred the belt to the chain on account of its smoothness, but improvements in all-chain transmission were rapid and by the mid-1920s all-chain drive was clearly in the ascendancy.

So too were well-designed countershaft gearboxes, although a number of the cheaper machines only offered two speeds at first. Four speeds were available in a few instances, but the most significant development was the positive-stop foot-change introduced by Velocette in 1928, though hand-change continued in wide use until the mid-1930s or so. The majority of motorcyclists made use of acetylene lighting, but the Americans had long ago shown the way to electric lighting, which was entirely satisfactory for motorcycles. The more expensive British machines followed suit, though for many years this refinement cost extra.

Improved performance brought the need for better brakes. The old stirrup brake of pedal-cycle origin was a pretty useless device, and indeed, the dummy belt-rim brake was little better. As the 1920s progressed, internal expanding hub brakes were more extensively used, while the change from the old narrow-section beaded-edge tyres to the wider low-pressure pattern was a significant help.

With rare exceptions, most frames were rigid. Only the front forks were sprung, but by the close of the 1930s, rear suspension and greatly improved front fork designs were evident. The coming of the cheap and reliable small car, heralded by the remarkable Austin Seven of 1922, beguiled many away from the ranks of touring and family motorcyclists. This was still more noticeable when small cars with saloon bodies were cheaply available, and so the greatest bugbear of the family motorcyclist was removed. However, there were still many diehards to whom the idea of motoring in a 'fug-box' was unpalatable.

Of all road users, perhaps it was the motorcyclists who were most often technically knowledgeable, friendly and possessed of a great sense of camaraderie. To a young man of the period, dreams were centred on a Norton, a Rudge or a Velocette (for the Land of the Rising Sun was far over the motorcycle horizon then). There were no 'Hell's Angels' connotations, and he learnt a respect for machinery, for the road, and for other road users that stood him in good stead on two, three or four wheels.

No event was held in higher esteem or exerted a greater influence on sporting motorcycles than the incomparable Tourist Trophy races, held in the Isle of Man since 1907 and revived after the First World War in 1920. The inter-war period saw the increase in classes eligible for these races and the introduction of the Amateur TT, which later grew into the Manx Grand Prix. Before the RAC ban in 1925, there were innumerable sprint events on the public roads. Sand-racing provided a popular alternative, and trials courses tended to become more and more 'off the road' in order to provide tough enough tests for men and machines. The late 1920s saw the rise of a new sport for motorcycles – the 'dirt-track' or 'speedway' – which soon attracted a very big and enthusiastic following, its star performers regarded in much the same light as today's star footballers.

In all these competitive elements, as in touring, the British motorcycle still held supreme, though in the late 1930s opposition from continental makers was very real and must have given some concern for the future.

*Right:* George Dance, one of Sunbeam's works riders, established a formidable reputation for success in speed events and trials, where he gained innumerable trophies for best performance of the day. He is seen here, in a white sweater, beside his early ohv sprint Sunbeam at a Welsh event, as usual with admirers around him. (*The Dance Archives*)

*Below:* The two-cylinder, two-stroke, two-speed Scott was a distinctive machine that earned a devoted following. Cooling was by water, the radiator below the steering head so as to catch the benefits of the slipstream. (*G. S. Boston*)

*Above:* A group of Carmarthenshire-registered bikes of the early 1920s, with BSA and Ariel machines.

*Opposite:* A very early Cotton, made by the individualistic Gloucester firm in *c.* 1922. This is one of the few early ones to be fitted with the Villiers two-stroke engine and the early form of front forks.

His and hers! This BSA combination is seen in a pleasantly rural location. In all probability, the lady occupied the sidecar more often than the saddle.

A BSA sidecar outfit features in this late 1920s family photograph. This bike wears a Wolverhampton mark (DA).

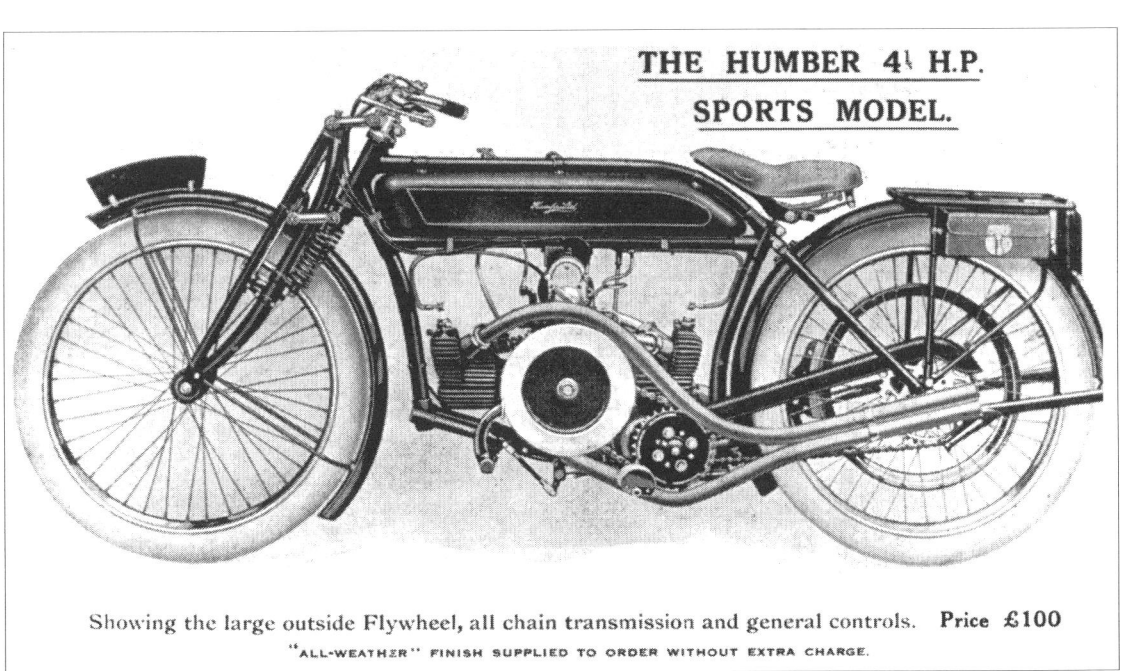

Humber was an old hand in the motorcycle industry, having made them from the start of the century until the Rootes takeover. This dates from the 1920s. (*The Humber Register*)

The touring model of the 4½-hp Humber is paired with a commodious and weather-proof sidecar – ideal for the family man. (*The Humber Register*)

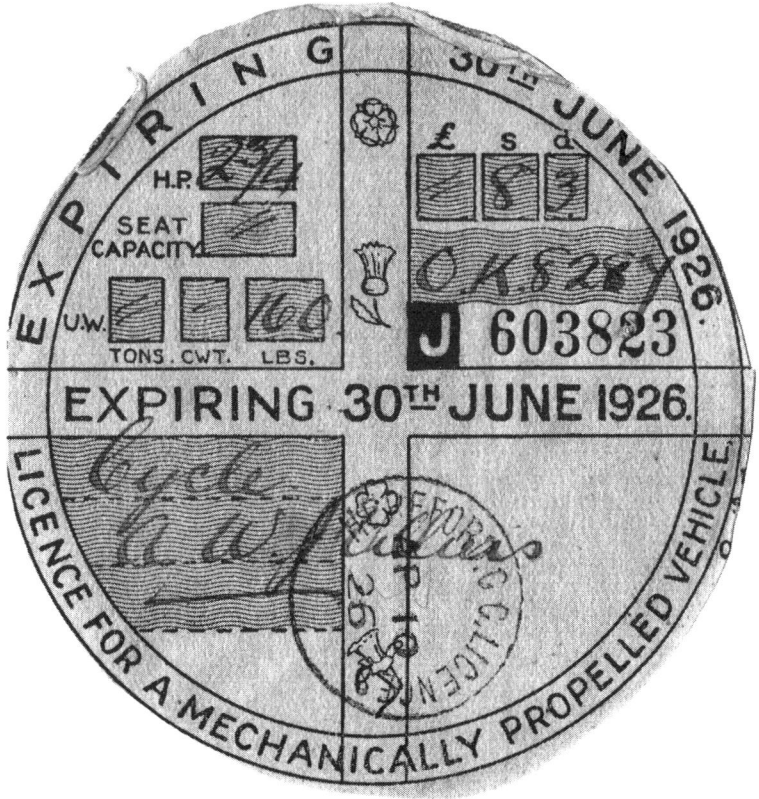

*Above and right:* As the licence reveals, this AWJ (A. W. James, not to be confused with A. J. Wheaton of Exeter, and the AJW) was originally fitted with a 250 cc Villiers two-stroke engine. The picture, however, shows it with a 770 cc V-twin engine, which, with the very primitive braking available, must have made it a very lethal machine.

To strap the bike to the running-board of a car was a favourite way to take it and the family to events. The bike is an Excelsior, the car a Cubitt.

*Opposite above:* This AJS was registered as FO 2336 (Radnorshire) on 7 February 1929. Here it is portrayed in Aymestrey, Herefordshire, when almost new. (*Leintwardine Local History Society*)

*Opposite below:* The 2¾-hp Humber in side-valve, overhead valve, and latterly ohc form was the mainstay of Humber's motorcycle production until motorcycles were phased out at the time of the Rootes takeover. These bikes were very refined and beautifully made.

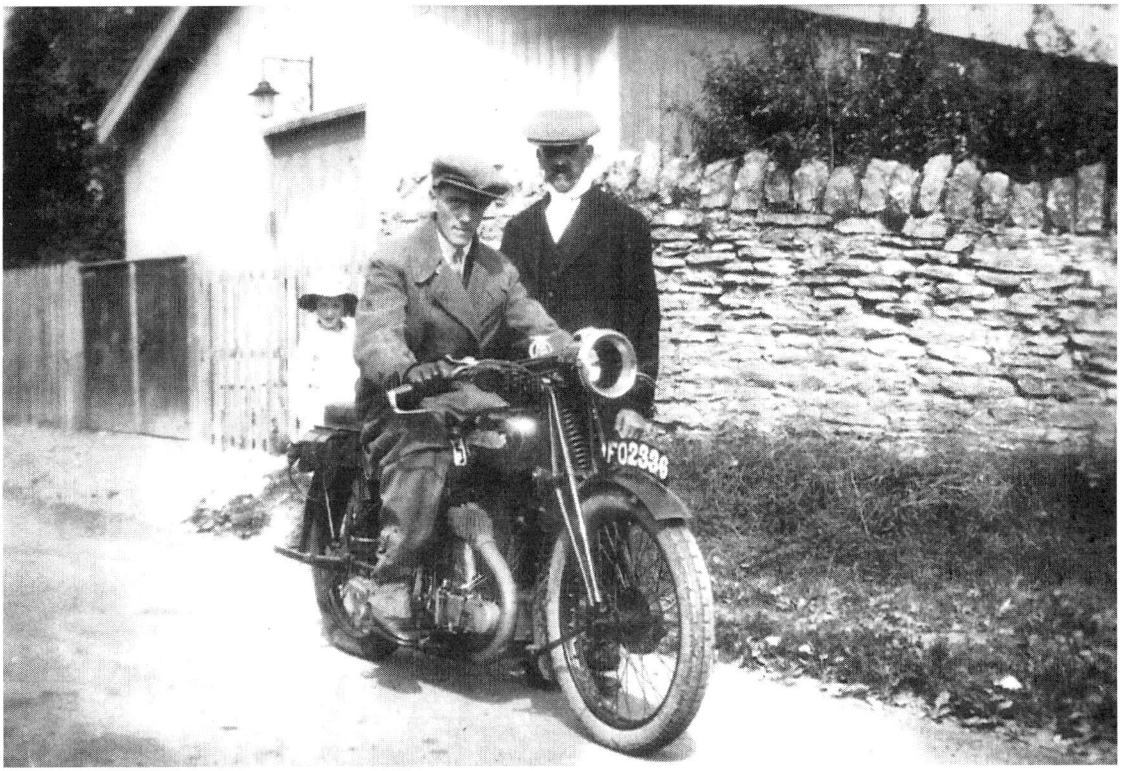
FO2336

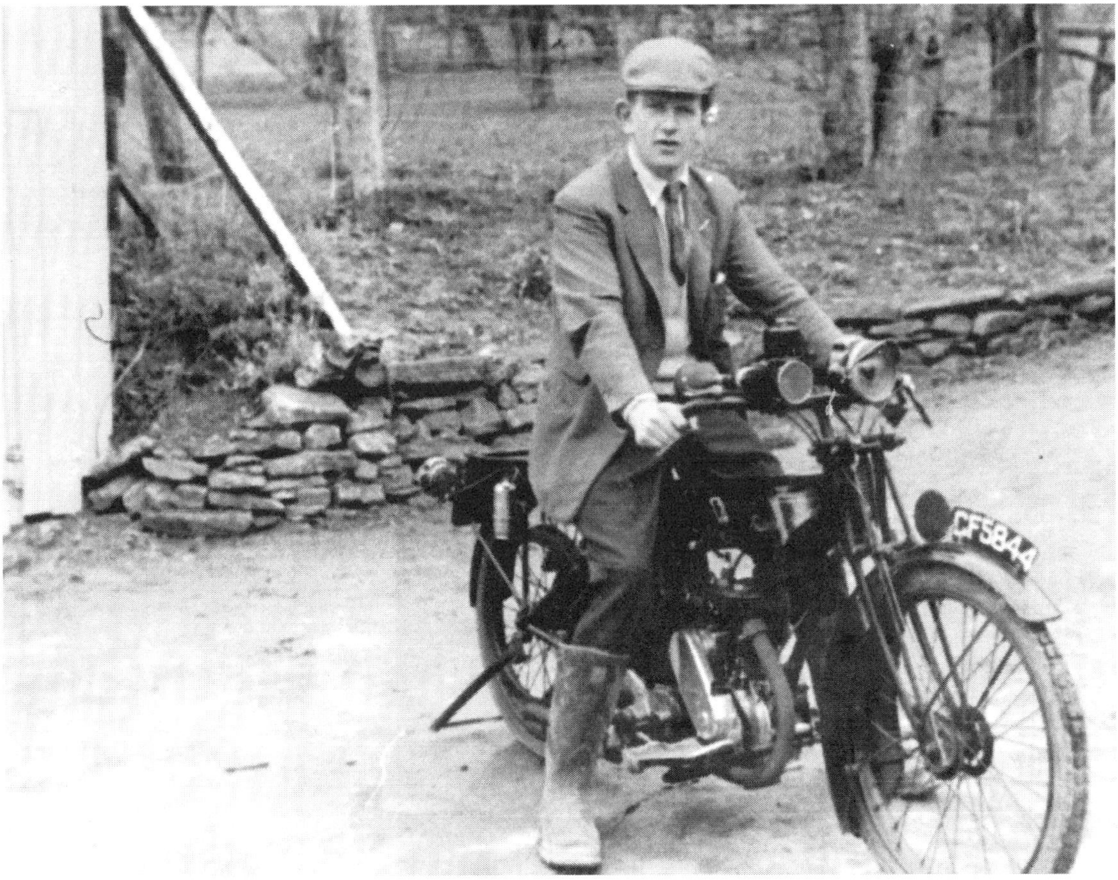
CF5844

This is an sv bike from a year later, 1926. As well as the acetylene light, a bulb horn, an AA badge and a small hand-klaxon are fitted to the handlebars. A basket is strapped to the carrier. Below it is the acetylene generator for the tail lamp.

Grass track events were very popular, and were usually carried out within a marked-out arena, as here. Motorcycle football was another popular variant.

Here is a very sporting ohv New Imperial with a Birmingham 'OH' plate. There is a Birmingham 'OP' plate in the background.

*Above:* Rosedale Abbey Bank was a notorious Yorkshire ascent that by 1927 had tapes laid to confine the competition to the worst part of the 'surface', as here. It was always a crowd puller.

*Left:* A fine big-twin AJS combination carries a Worcester mark (FK). Note the hood folded on the side-car, the spare wheel and the massive acetylene lighting set. Presumably the young lady on the fence occupied the sidecar, or perhaps the pillion. (*G. D. Smith*)

# 2
# CYCLECARS & BABIES

A 1920s joke in that venerable journal *Punch* read, 'I can't come out yet, dear, I'm washing the baby,' and illustrated the young wife attending to the ablutions of the Baby car in the bath. Perhaps the Austin Seven was the first British car to occupy a place in the affections of the British public akin to that of the legendary Model T Ford, the 'Tin Lizzie', in America. It was certainly a landmark in motoring history.

The cyclecar was much more closely related to the motorcycle, and had enjoyed its first boom from about 1912. Usually powered by an air-cooled motorcycle engine, most cyclecars were crude in the extreme, but achieved a decent performance thanks to a good power-to-weight ratio. The more sporting cyclecars offered performance and economy, with marginally less exposure to the elements than a motorcycle. The better of them, such as the GN and the Morgan, had an appeal that caused them to survive, if not prosper, for a longer period than those whose only virtues were low initial cost and economy of operation.

Cyclecars underwent a revival in the years immediately after the 1918 Armistice, first because demand for anything that would motor was so great, and secondly because prices rose alarmingly and the cyclecar was about the cheapest available to an undemanding public. But what really killed the breed was the advent of the Austin Seven in 1922. Considered a joke at first, the 'Baby' Austin, as it soon came to be affectionately termed, was a large car in miniature. It even boasted minuscule four-wheel brakes whose stopping power was more technical than actual. But it was well built of first-class materials and had a water-cooled four-cylinder engine, electric lighting and, shortly after its introduction, electric starting as well. It also boasted adequate weather protection and ample space for two adults and two children or one child and luggage, and it was inexpensive in first cost and upkeep. One could say that it was the Baby that changed motoring, if not overnight, then certainly within the decade. A saloon-bodied version was available from May 1926.

Austin's greatest rival, Morris, entered the baby car market in 1929 with the Morris Minor – at first with an overhead camshaft engine, which was the inspiration for Cecil Kimber's MG Midget, which itself sparked off a remarkable run of sports cars. Triumph brought out the Super Seven, surprisingly with hydraulic four-wheel brakes, and, rather in a class of its own, the Jowett from Yorkshire carried remarkably commodious bodywork on its longer chassis and always relied on two cylinders until 1936, when Jowett introduced a flat-four and moved out of the 'baby' field.

A few others had tried to break into this market, but within a short time their babies tended to put on power and weight and thus, strictly speaking, move out of that particular field. But none enjoyed the success or the affection of the public that attended the Austin Seven, which, though refined and updated, did not finally go out of production until 1938. Its phenomenal success in all forms of motoring competition from trials to out-and-out racing is another story, but certainly one that vindicates a remarkably inspired design. The Austin Seven, more than any other car, killed the cyclecar stone dead.

Morgan of Malvern was by far the most competition-orientated of the three-wheeler cyclecars of the 1920s and '30s. Here a JAP-engined model poses with some typical 1920s ladies. (*Berrows Newspapers*)

This early Morgan cyclecar, painted green/black, was first registered in Monmouthshire but is here portrayed in Kilpeck, one of Herefordshire's many attractive villages.

*Left:* The child of today is the motorist of tomorrow. It is a sobering thought that if this proud youngster's pedal-car came on the market today, it would doubtless fetch enough money to buy him a very handsome new grown-up car! (*Marshall, Harrison & Baldwin*)

*Below:* The Castle-Three Runabout was an attempt by a small firm to 'civilise' the cyclecar image. The design had a number of good points, but the transmission caused serious setbacks which, with other difficulties, caused manufacture to stop after only some 350 had been completed. It was also unfortunate that, as a three-wheeler, the weight of the car should have greatly exceeded the limit that would qualify it for the reduced rate of tax. Much was made of the fact that all wheels were quickly interchangeable, and that a water-cooled four-cylinder engine was used. (*S. F. Sapp*)

An elderly gentleman at the controls of a very sporting GN. Godfrey and Nash, the progenitors of the GN, were both of highly sporting dispositions and their product, which later developed into the Frazer Nash, was one of the most speedy and popular of the many cyclecars that were a feature of the early 1920s. (*E. Widgery*)

The LSD was a singularly ugly three-wheeler made from 1920 to 1924 by Sykes & Sugden in very small numbers. It was the butt of many jokes that it wasn't worth pence – never mind pounds or shillings. Here, it is set up at a display stand at a show. (*B. K. Goodman*)

A twin-cylinder air-cooled Rover Eight is dwarfed by the landaulette (probably a Daimler, judging by those wooden slats protecting the petrol tank) alongside it on a Scottish ferry. Even the rather minimal equipment of a typical early 1920s small car of this sort was better than that of its nearest rival, the motorcycle combination. (*J. Ahern/D. Irvine*)

Never too old to mind the Baby! The Austin Seven, for all its peccadilloes, was an inspired design that did more for the cause of motoring for the masses than any car other, perhaps, than the Model T of Henry Ford. This 1925 Chummy, in pristine condition, is obviously the pride and joy of its elderly owner.

Gordon England himself is snugly seated in an early version of his high-performance 'Brooklands' Austin Seven, appropriately enough in the paddock at Brooklands. Sir Herbert Austin's Baby was to develop into a very potent infant indeed, in the hands of the racing specialists.

*Opposite above:* Even quite humble cars competed in club events at Brooklands. This Austin Seven 'top hat' saloon takes part in the JCC's High Speed Reliability Trial on 18 June 1927. The Austin is followed by a Frazer Nash and a Ceirano. An unfortunate AC lies ditched beside the road.

*Opposite below:* The penultimate design in the development of the Austin Seven as a racer, this neat little side-valver made its first appearance at Shelsley Walsh on 18 May 1935. Walter Baumer is at the wheel of this one. The following year saw the introduction of the twin-overhead camshaft version developed by Murray Jamieson – a far cry indeed from the funny little Baby of 1922. (*J. Ahern/D. Irvine*)

A pretty little Swallow-bodied Austin Seven. Although little better in actual performance than the standard versions, these Swallow-bodied cars were much more attractively bodied and turned out, and had a great popular appeal.

# 3
# GOING FOR A SPIN

In the early years of the inter-war period, the emphasis in motor touring, or just motoring, was for the most part that it was undertaken with due deliberation; one did not jump into the car and immediately rush off to one's destination, be it near or far. Why not? Well, we shall see that deliberation was in part an attitude of mind, in part enjoined by the motorcar itself.

First, there was the starting procedure, a ritual indeed, and if the motor did not start, then one repeated the ritual. Most cars had their individual whims, with which a sensible owner would soon learn to come to terms. Even when one enjoyed the luxury of a self-starter (not by any means universal in the early 1920s, but soon becoming a *sine qua non*), one freed the engine first on the handle to reduce the load imposed on the starter motor and battery.

But wait. One still should not actually be off on one's journey, for the motor must be allowed to warm up a little before it is expected to travel under load. Oils were less universally adaptable then than now. Even when one did get under way, one was careful not to open the throttle excessively, especially in the indirect gears, until the motor had thoroughly warmed up. Soon one was bowling along the road at, perhaps, 20 mph (still the legal limit).

Open touring cars predominated, either in four- or five-seater form or the then-popular two-seater and dickey. The dickey, meant as an occasional accommodation, varied enormously in its appointments (or lack of them), and was passable in fine weather but excruciating in bad. At all times it was somewhat unsociable, since it was virtually impossible to communicate with those in front. But tourer or two-seater, the hood would be down more often than not, the top panel of the windscreen would be slightly open to reduce backdraught, and all aboard would be well wrapped up, except in the warmest weather. In Britain's fickle climate, one often had to consider the possibility of being cold or wet. To stop and erect the hood was to risk getting wetter than to motor on in the hope that the rain would diminish or cease altogether. The much-vaunted 'one-man' hood might well take five minutes to erect – it involved undoing the hood cover and sundry straps and clips, persuading it out of its folds, pulling at its joints to stretch the fabric gratefully over the screen pillars, and nursing several sore fingers.

In really wet weather, of course, the hood was up and the sidecurtains too. The noise inside the car immediately increased, and was added to by the innumerable scratchings, squeaks, groans and windy flappings of the large area of best double-duck that did its best to keep one dry. Luggage? Whether the luggage was in the dry or not depended on whether one was fussy. An unoccupied dickey seat was an excellent stowage in the dry, and was often so laden with the general impedimenta of motoring that it was well-nigh impossible to accommodate extra passengers. Alternatively, most tourers had ample space between the front and rear seats in which luggage could be placed, and most commonly of all there was the luggage grid at the rear, exposed to the elements. The luggage had either to be covered with a waterproof securely lashed down, or one could have a purpose-built trunk.

The owner-driver was expected to have a reasonable mechanical knowledge; enough, anyway, to cope with common minor breakdowns on the road, and with this in mind a toolkit was carried in the car. All manufacturers provided one as a matter of course, though its contents varied. Humbers, representative of the better-quality touring cars of the time, came with a toolkit of over forty items, but not all makers were as generous.

In the early 1920s, most cars lacked four-wheel brakes; speeds on the whole were low and braking distances long. If one's car did have the newfangled four-wheel brakes, it was prudent to wear a red warning triangle on the rear of the car as advice of the car's allegedly superior stopping power to those astern. Most drivers were aware of the limitations of current braking systems. They slowed when descending steep hills and contrived to use the brakes only in emergencies or to bring the car to a stop, methods of driving that also helped to lessen the likelihood of 'the dreaded sideslip', a danger that had been ingrained into motorists almost from the first. Yes, motoring for the average motorist of the 1920s was full of deliberation.

Far removed from the cyclecar image, this Silver Ghost Rolls-Royce shows motoring at the other end of the spectrum and is the embodiment of refinement. Here is a car that could cope with any occasion, from the formal to the Grand Tour, without causing a moment's misgiving. (*M. Dowty*)

This is no Rolls-Royce, although you could be forgiven for thinking so. It is a Roamer, an American car of the early 1920s powered by a 5-litre engine. (*B. K. Goodman*)

Simple but balanced, the dashboard of this 1919 Horstman is typical of a light car of this time. Unique, however, is the prominent kick-starter in the centre. If its operation was highly hazardous to one's shin, at least there was no need to get out of the car. (*T. H. D. Attewell*)

America's motor industry achieved mass production long before that of this country, and the Chevrolet seen here is typical of the simple and rugged American touring car imports of the early 1920s. This five-seater touring car undercut the Morris Cowley by quite a few pounds, but its £22 annual tax (as against £12 for the Morris) and its heavier petrol consumption had to be borne in mind. (*National Library of Wales*)

This Worcestershire-registered 18-hp Essex tourer was a much-travelled car; it covered a considerable mileage at home and abroad.

This Herefordshire gentleman stands beside his brand-new 20-hp Waverley cabriolet. It wears a Herefordshire Trade Plate, '0010 CJ', red lettering on a white background. Note the beautifully wrapped spare tyre.

The driver poses separately with the same charming cabriolet of the early 1920s. Detachable rims were unusual on cars of other than American origin at this date, but could be obtained at a customer's request, even on a Rolls-Royce.

This very attractive special-bodied Vauxhall 30/98 was used for extended continental tours by its enthusiastic owner. (*G. S. Boston*)

*Opposite above:* There is no mistaking the well-known 'Bullnose', though this one has a boot tied round its radiator cap. With the floral buttonholes of the passengers, this suggests wedding festivities. (*National Library of Wales*)

*Opposite below:* A quiet spin down a country lane in summer with a *c.* 1924 11.4 Humber. Many such lanes survived with a similar surface devoid of tarmac for another decade or more. The Humber was a typical good-quality medium touring car, characteristic of the period before saloons began to outdo open cars in popular favour. For inclement weather, the Humber's weather equipment was better than most. (*M. Dowty*)

41

42

In this quiet 1920s scene, the Swan Inn at Newland near Malvern hosts a Morgan on the left, a Talbot on the right, and three motorcycles. (*Norman May's Studio Ltd*)

*Opposite above:* A Rover of c. 1924 demonstrates the virtues typical of its kind – roominess and adequate weather protection. Rovers were early users of sidescreens opening with the doors.

*Opposite below:* The Malvern firm of Santler's last effort at car production was this three-wheeler, known as the Santler Rushabout. Its appearance and its mechanical features were strongly reminiscent of the much better known Morgans of Malvern. Fewer than twenty of these cars were built, some appearing with a light delivery-van body.

Malvern's Morgan trike. This example, a water-cooled Aero model, was one of the most attractive and successful of the factory's cars.

*Opposite above:* Reputed to be the only make of car to have been advertised in *The Church Times*, Leslie Hounsfield's highly unorthodox utility car, the Trojan, certainly appealed to orthodox churchmen, for it was the choice of many clerics. Its most optimistic top speed would not have alarmed the most timorous parishioner and it could withstand the cruelest ill-treatment with Christian meekness and fortitude. This example wears the pneumatic tyres that were available as an option for those who could not quite stomach the solids that were standard wear on the majority of Trojans.

*Opposite below:* This view of a 1921 Humber 'Ten', which the RAC rated at 11.4-hp, reveals many features typical of motoring in this period. The upper panel of the screen is slightly open because this reduced the backdraught when the hood was down (which it was, more often than not). The mounting of the spare wheel precludes the use of a door on the driver's side. The dickey-seat, unsociable at the best of times, is, however, comfortably upholstered and provided with arm-rests and the panel in front of it could be raised to any angle to deflect the wind. (*The Humber Register*)

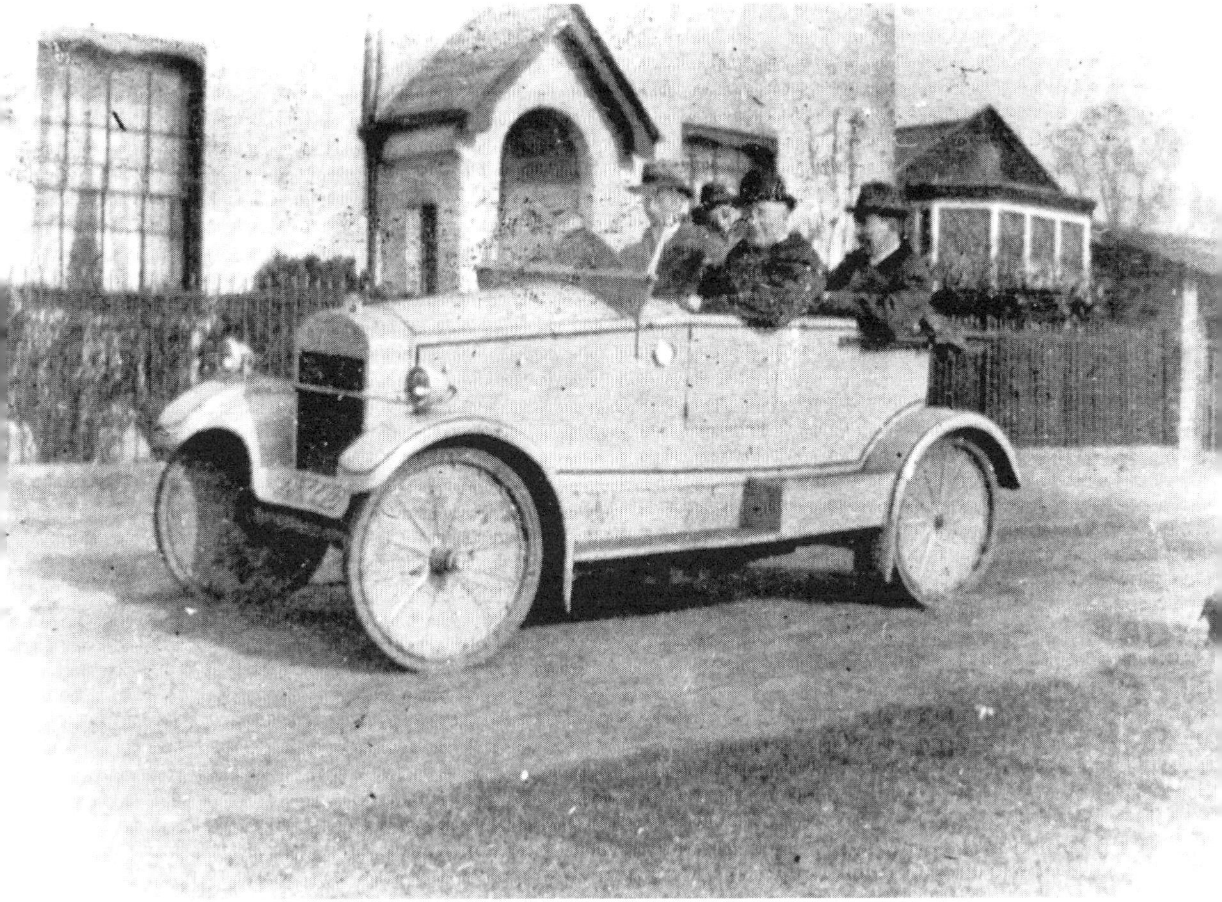

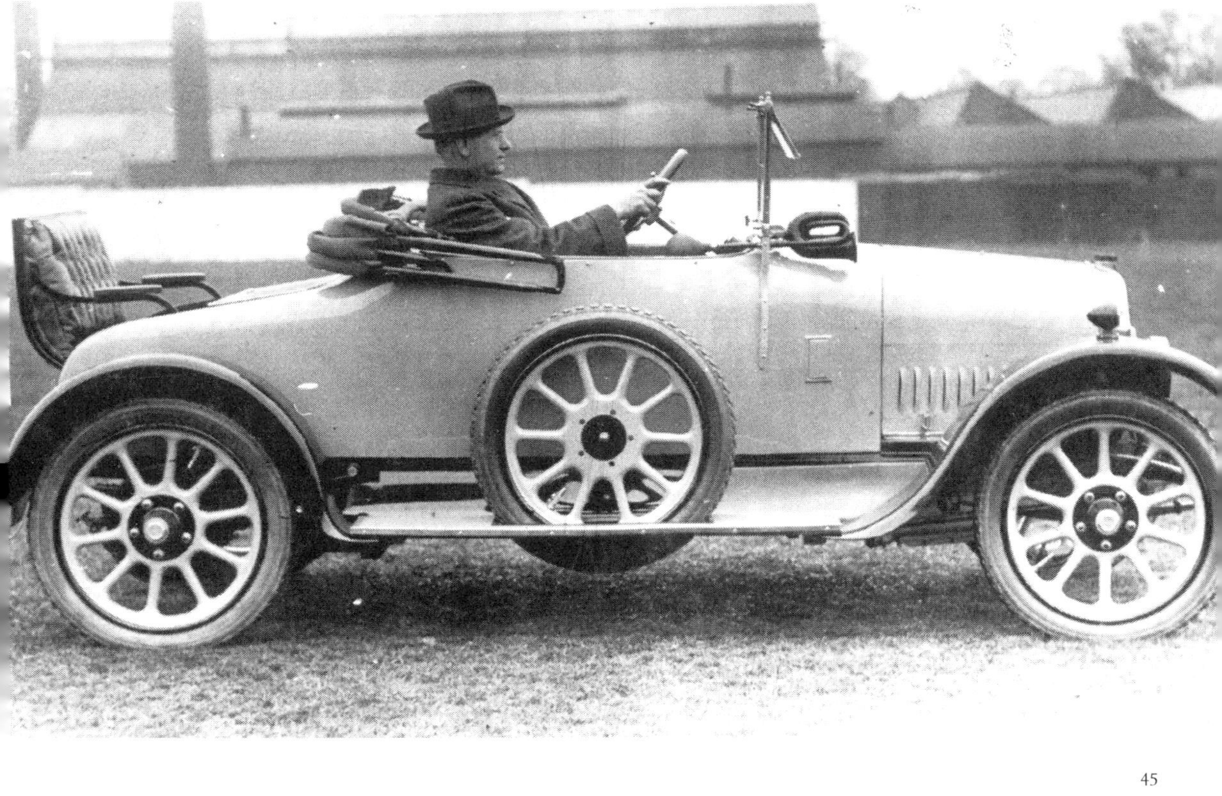

Perhaps not 'the Hon. Bertie' himself, as in the maker's advertisements, but no doubt the driver of this splendid Alvis 12/50 Super-Sports would agree with that fictional hero that 'She's some car, believe me.' (*National Library of Wales*)

Here is a delightful Aston Martin awaiting its owner. This car was shown at a 1925 show just before the sad demise of Lionel Martin's old company. (*N. F. Murray*)

A cheerful party of youngsters photographed aboard an Anzani-engined Frazer Nash during a summer holiday. The Frazer Nash, a make that perpetuated chain transmission until the late 1930s, had an uncompromisingly sporting emphasis and an individuality to which it was impossible to be indifferent. It inspired either an almost fanatical affection or an equally acute dislike. The young man at the wheel obviously subscribes to the former view! (*H. G. Pitt*)

A six-cylinder 24/90 Straker-Squire halts beneath the dappled shade of a wayside tree. This massively built and finely proportioned car owed something in its bevel-driven overhead camshaft design to earlier Mercedes practice, but was in fact the brainchild of the late Sir Roy Fedden. (*G. F. Lomas*)

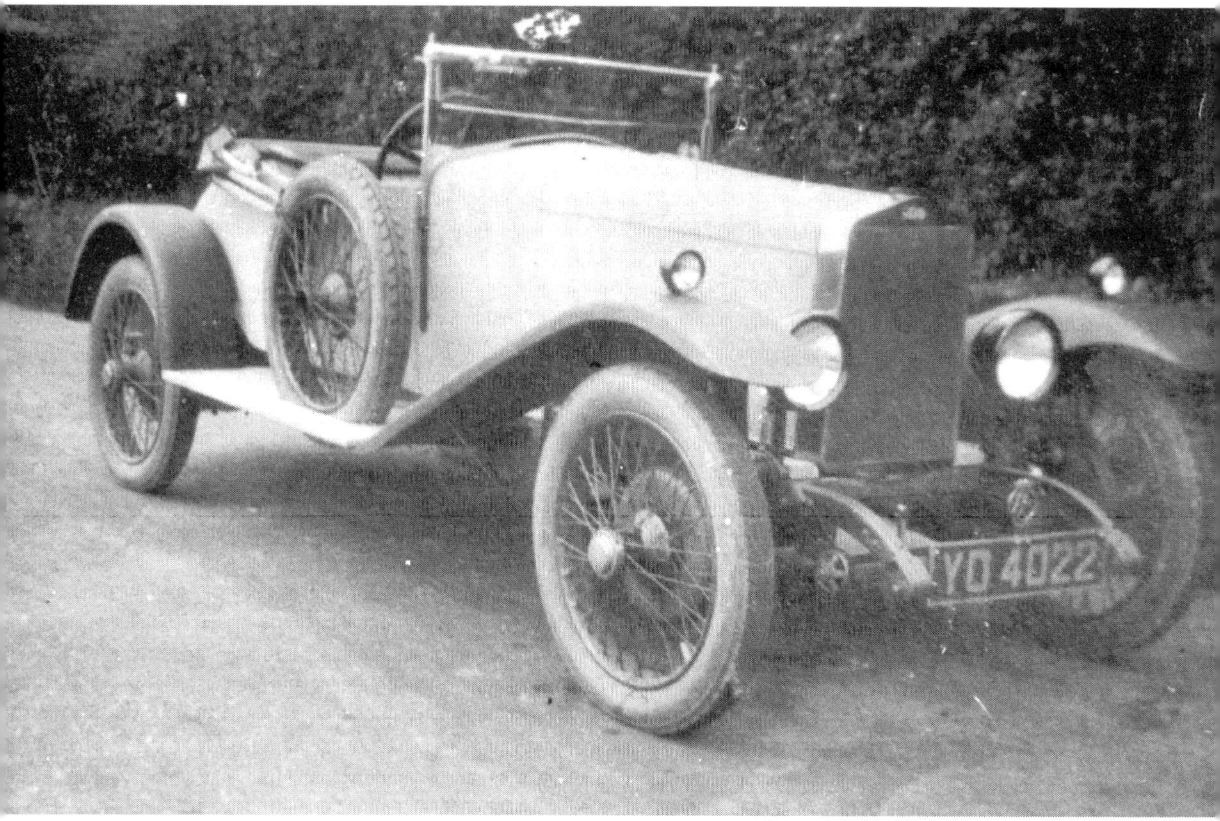
YO 4022

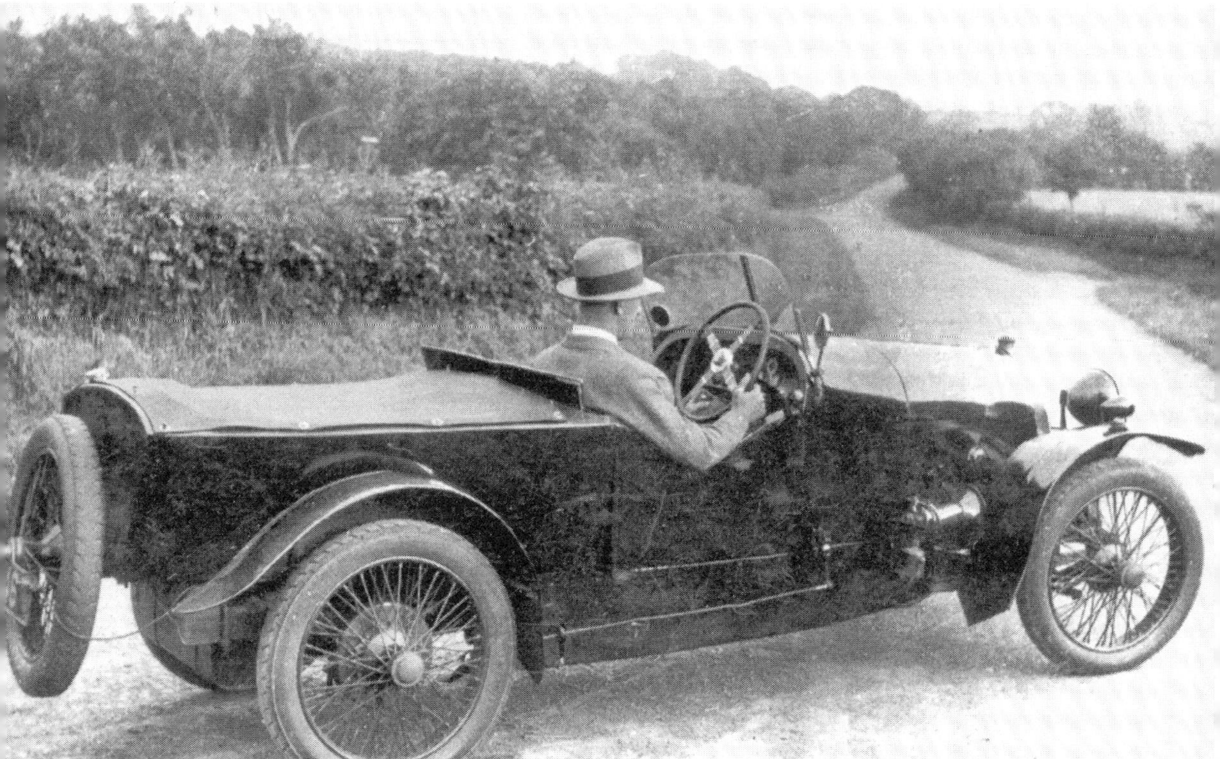

Photographed on a sunny day in Malvern, a Standard and a 14/40 Vauxhall thread their way cautiously down a steeply graded street; cautiously not because of traffic but because the Standard at least is not provided with four-wheel brakes – a deficiency that the Vauxhall probably shares. (*Norman May's Studio's Ltd*)

*Opposite above:* This very rare car, a 2-litre Arab of 1926, was purchased as a chassis and then had this simple but typically British two-seater body made for it, at a cost of £60. Later it had a stylish fabric coupé body built for it, and even later it acquired a body from a 30/98 Vauxhall. Only about a dozen Arabs were made, but they were cars of a distinguished pedigree and of considerable potential. (*L. E. van Moppes*)

*Opposite below:* This Bugatti Brescia *modifié* sets out for a summer spin around the leafy lanes of Herefordshire. (*Pritchard, Hereford*)

Photographed in August 1928, this Bean 12-hp tourer poses near Lichfield. Grown out of the Perry, the Bean was intended for production on a massive scale, but optimistic early target figures were never realised, matters grew worse, and no Bean cars were made after 1929. It was thoughtful to include the chauffeur in this family-album picture. (*Miss A. Wilkinson*)

Photographed here is Mrs Bennett, who, with her husband the Revd G. Bennett, embarked on a very adventurous trip from Winchester to the far north of Scotland with a tiny German car, a Piccolo, in 1906. Mrs Bennett remained a keen motorist and is seen here with her 1920 Humber 10-hp two-seater. (*Mrs G. Bennett*)

*Above:* A singularly happy marriage between a quality American chassis, the Lincoln V8, and nicely proportioned and pleasingly unfussy British coachwork. The Lincoln greyhound leaps enticingly forward from the radiator cap and a padlock secures the spare wheel. (*M. Dowty*)

*Right:* A British-owned 2-litre Metallurgique of semi-sporting mien, and boasting a single overhead camshaft engine, sets off across the roads of France on its way to Switzerland in August 1926. This famous Belgian make was absorbed by its compatriot, Minerva, in the following year. (*A. J. Ahern/D. Irvine*)

This fine 3-litre Invicta tackles one of the remoter parts of the London-Edinburgh Trial in the late 1920s. (*A. J. Ahern/D. Irvine*)

This handsome Crossley 20/70 sports tourer takes a smiling Yorkshire family for a spin on the moors of that county in the mid-1920s. (*Mrs G. Moore*)

# 4
# MOTORING... ALMOST FOR THE MASSES

Prior to about 1925, the closed car was largely reserved for formal occasions or town use, but as performance improved so that even the smallest cars could carry closed bodywork, and as new techniques of mass production, copied from America, enabled closed bodywork to be produced cheaply, so fashion and our fickle climate brought the closed car to the fore. In 1925 the majority of makers turned out probably five or six times as many open cars as closed ones; ten years later, the ratio was reversed. The sporting motorist clung most consistently to open sports cars, but even he was being tempted away by sports saloons and sports coupés by the mid-1930s.

Early closed bodywork was tall, heavy and expensive, and early mass-produced closed cars were boxy, four-square and stark in their appointments. As the 1920s drew to a close, there was a revulsion against this angularity of outline, which at first produced a period of singularly unattractive high-waisted fabric-finished saloons in a misguided attempt to diminish the appearance of height and, less misguidedly, to reduce weight. The novel and patented Weymann system of silent fabric-covered construction was in a class of its own and often looked very handsome, particularly on a large chassis. Unfortunately, it had many cheap and nasty imitators who used inferior materials and could not incorporate the salient design features without falling foul of the patents. Luckily they were short-lived; their shoddiness ensured it. Meanwhile, great improvements were being made in mass-production techniques, so that by the mid-1930s saloon cars were no longer tall and angular but lower and more rounded in outline.

No sooner had the closed car overtaken the open car in popularity than with typical perversity its users wanted more sun and air, and the sunshine roof became all the rage. Mechanically, many changes were on the way, too. Much effort was directed towards simpler gear-changing. Armstrong Siddeley popularised the 'self-change' pre-selector gearbox, and to this Daimler added the fluid-flywheel. In 1931, Vauxhall became the first British makers to introduce synchromesh with their Cadet. Four-wheel brakes were the rule, not the exception, and hydraulic operation was on the increase. Coil ignition had virtually ousted the old magneto and gave easier starting but a greater dependence on the battery. This long-suffering component also had to cope with an increasing number of electrical items.

Two important safety features became legally obligatory. The first was the compulsory use of safety-glass windscreens, soon to spread to all glass; the second was compulsory third-party insurance – sensible legislation in view of the ever-increasing traffic. The relaxation of the old 20 mph speed limit did not mean an immediate free-for-all, for speed limits were widely imposed in built-up areas, giving rise to quantities of limit and derestriction signs that formed only a small part of a rapidly increasing jungle of motoring 'street furniture'. The depression years had sent a host of motor manufacturers to the wall, with the result that the 1930s saw a process of rationalisation of models from those makers that still struggled to survive.

Town and countryside were beginning to come to terms with mass motor mobility, but on the whole they were not very successful. The outbreak of war turned thoughts and energies into different channels and the problems that motoring of the 1930s raised were, perforce, shelved – only to rear their hydroid heads more urgently decades later.

Speed with elegance is typified in this shot of J. Lucas-Scudamore's 2LS Ballot from March 1923. (*J. Lucas-Scudamore*)

This Rolls-Royce Silver Ghost of the early 1920s reveals the legacy of Edwardian thinking in its tall landaulette coachwork, which gives ample room for formally dressed occupants. Even some of the coachwork styles on the 'New Phantom', which succeeded the Silver Ghost, were very similar.

Not an uncommon fate for elderly Rolls-Royces, this example has been rebodied as a shooting-brake for use on the Scottish estate of a wealthy family. Despite its more humble status, it is obviously very well cared for. (*F. Smith*)

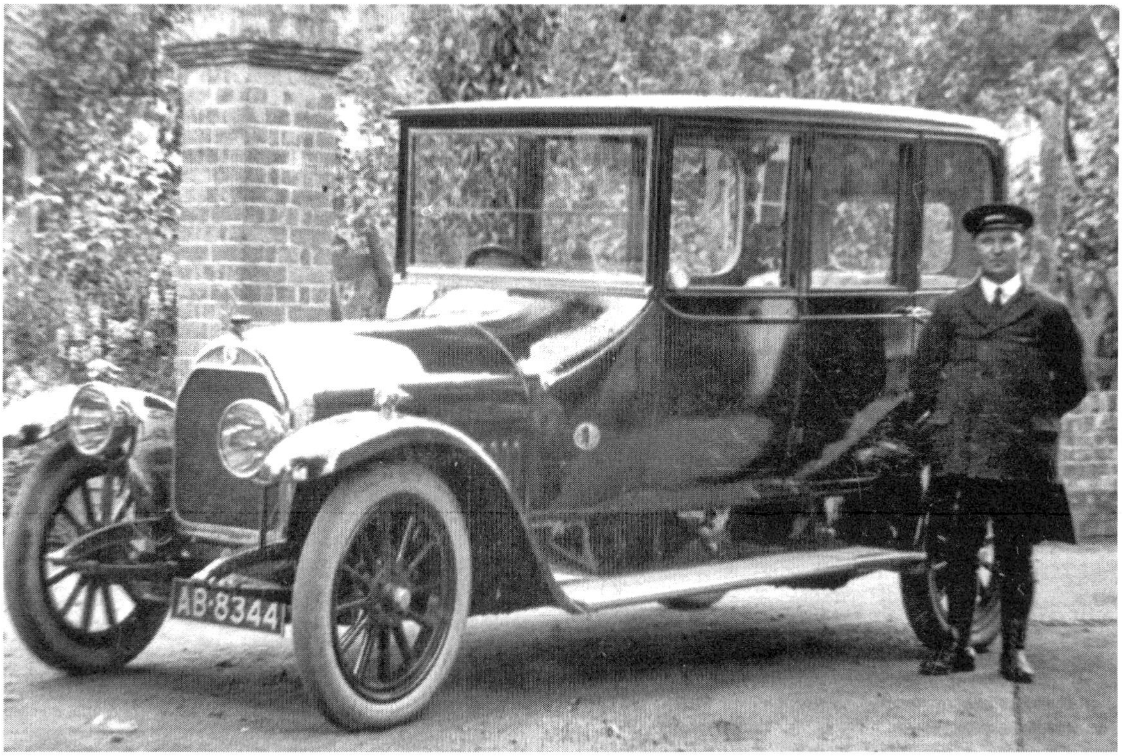
AB·8344

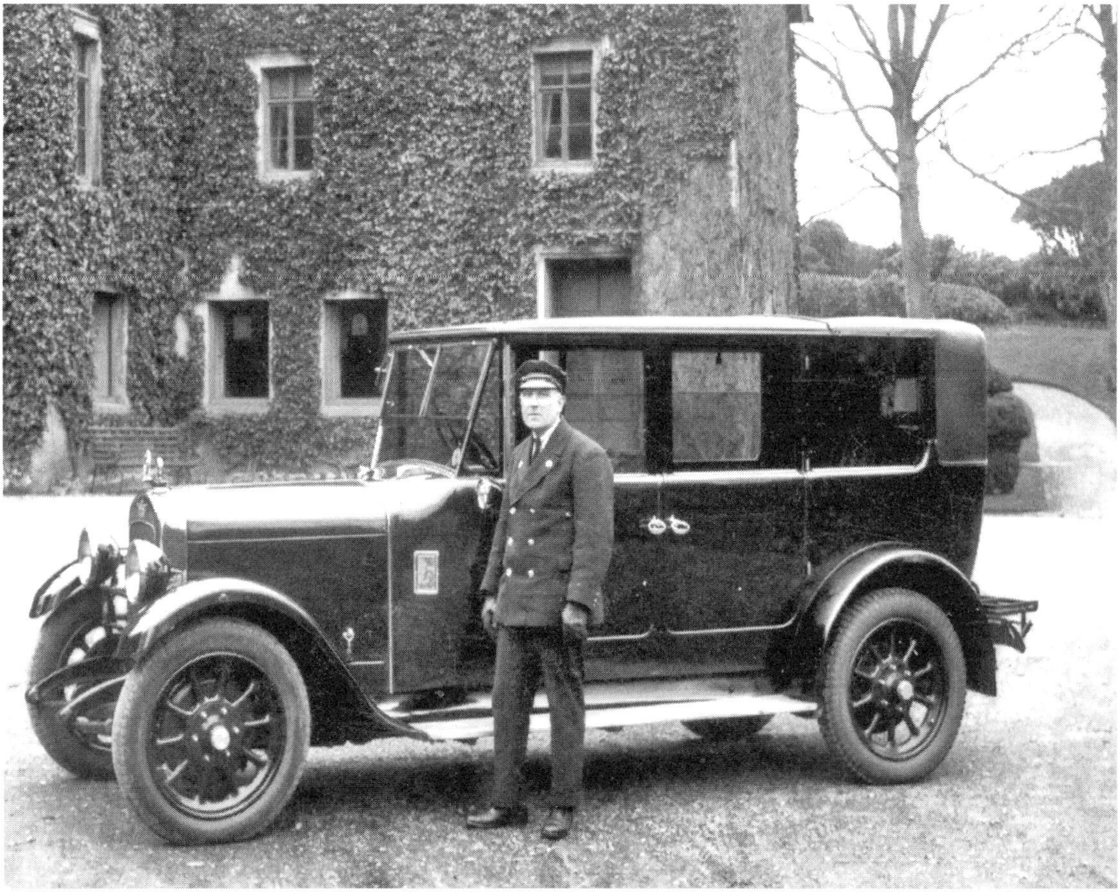

Daimlers, with their quiet but smoky sleeve-valve engines, were popular with those who valued comfort and silence above performance. In all probability this example is a hire car, for the muffler and cloth cap would scarcely have passed muster in private service.

*Opposite above:* Early 1920s tall saloons were a legacy from the Edwardian era. The saloon body on this chauffeur-driven Darracq carries only one door on the near side, so that access to the front passenger's seat would involve the seat swivelling. This was a less convenient method than the more usual one of providing two doors on the near side but only one on the off side – the driver then had to enter or leave the car by way of the front passenger's door. On the other hand, the method adopted here did enable the chauffeur to enter or leave the car without disturbing the front passenger.

*Opposite below:* The four-cylinder Austin Twenty made an admirable hire car, though this example is probably in private service. The driver has the sort of homely face that so ably complemented this worthy but unexciting car.

*Left:* This Bugatti, type Brescia Modifié, was used by a very keen Herefordshire owner in the late 1920s. It displays the characteristic pear-drop radiator. (*Pritchard, Hereford*)

*Below:* This commodious fabric saloon of *c.* 1928 is a 16/65 Lagonda, which, unlike the better-known and more sporting 2-litre, was a six-cylinder car with pushrod overhead valves. Most Lagondas were massively constructed, so the fabric body of this example does little to reduce a weight that limited performance to a maximum of 65 mph or so. A well-appointed car, it shared many chassis features of the 2-litre, including very effective and easily adjusted brakes. (*L. F. Barham*)

The 1920s and '30s were the heyday of the mascot. This Standard tourer boasts a very large and cheeky black cat for good luck.

Even quite humble cars were proud enough possessions for the new acquisition to be photographed with the family, like this 'Bullnose' Morris tourer of 1925/26.

*Left:* Practically unknown to Sassenachs, this car, with a hint of Riley about it, is the Little Scotsman of 1930, powered by the well-proven Meadows 4ED engine. One wonders how many of these saw the light of day, even north of the border. (*Marshall, Harris & Baldwin*)

*Below:* This handsome Austin 12/4 appears to have coachwork by an 'outside' coachbuilder – prettier than Austin's standard effort. With plenty of luggage, it appears to be ready to set out on a long journey.

This photograph, taken near Chedworth, Gloucestershire, shows a 1926 3-litre Bentley short chassis speed model with Vandan Plas coachwork, with the mark YM 2872.

This Citroën tourer with a Leeds registration is far from home in Devon in July 1923.

By the time of this shot, 1933, the General Motors influence at Vauxhall's Luton plant was total. The Light Six seen here was available with a 12-hp or 14-hp engine, and caused sales to leap gratifyingly upward. (*National Library of Wales*)

*Opposite above:* It doesn't look brand-new, but they're very proud of this 1937 Standard Flying 12 saloon nevertheless. If they managed to hang on to it until after the war, it would doubtless have sold for much more than the original purchase price. (*National Library of Wales*)

*Opposite below:* An old, established make, Riley picked a winner in the Nine, introduced for 1927. This 1934 Imp was one of their most attractive sports cars and was offered when the Riley Nine was at the height of a successful racing career. (*G. D. Smith*)

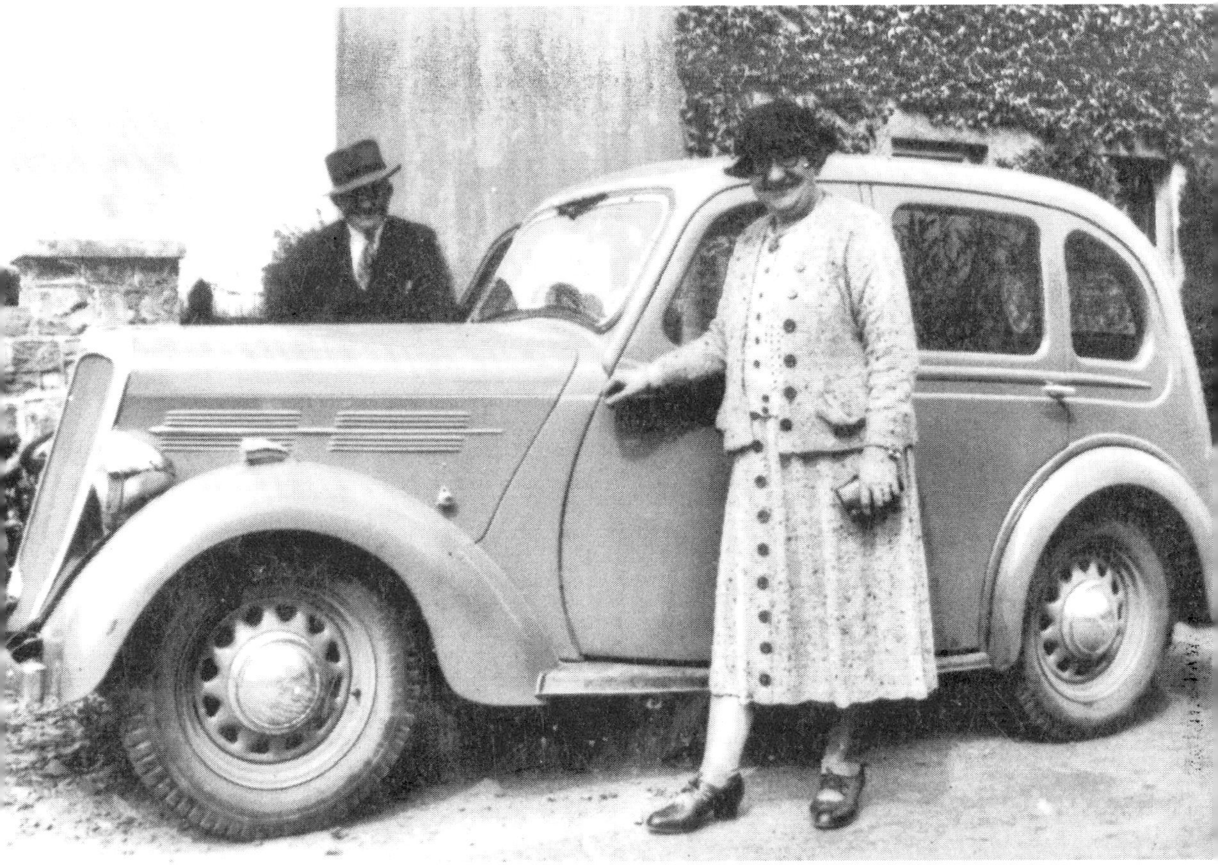

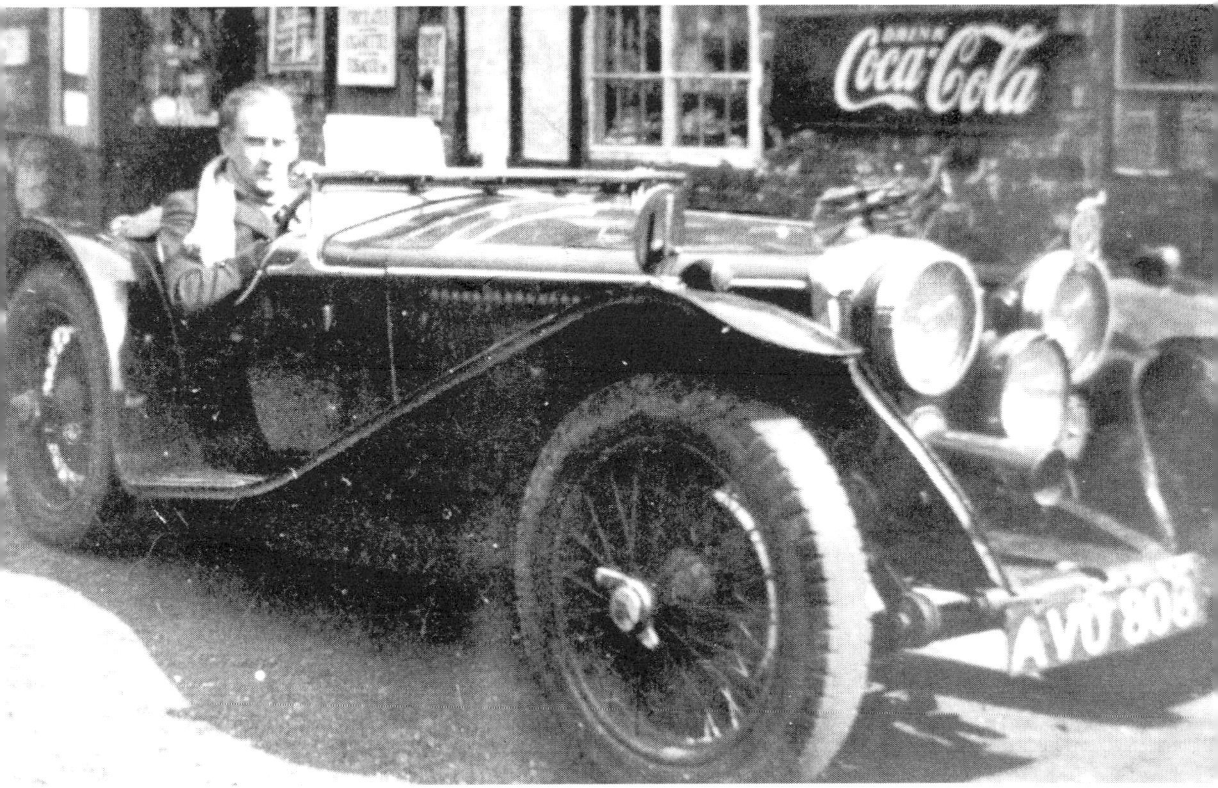
Coca-Cola

Two examples of the coachbuilders' art on quality chassis: a Minerva and an Invicta. The former was a wedding present from a groom to his bride, and the Invicta belonged to the same family of discerning motorists. (*W. H. Summers*)

Speed, comfort, looks and luxury summed up in this fine 6½-litre Bentley with Park Ward fixed-head coupé bodywork. In the days before modern ventilation systems, the openable screen was a boon in hot weather and even more so in thick fog. (*J. D. Leathley*)

The acme of the mid-1930s Teutonic image, this fine Horch coupé suggests power and speed in every line. Aptly, for its owner is Hans Stück von Villiez, racing motorist and hill-climb champion, who is seen talking to the Secretary of the Midland Automobile Club after that club's Shelsley Walsh meeting of June 1936. (*Midland AC*)

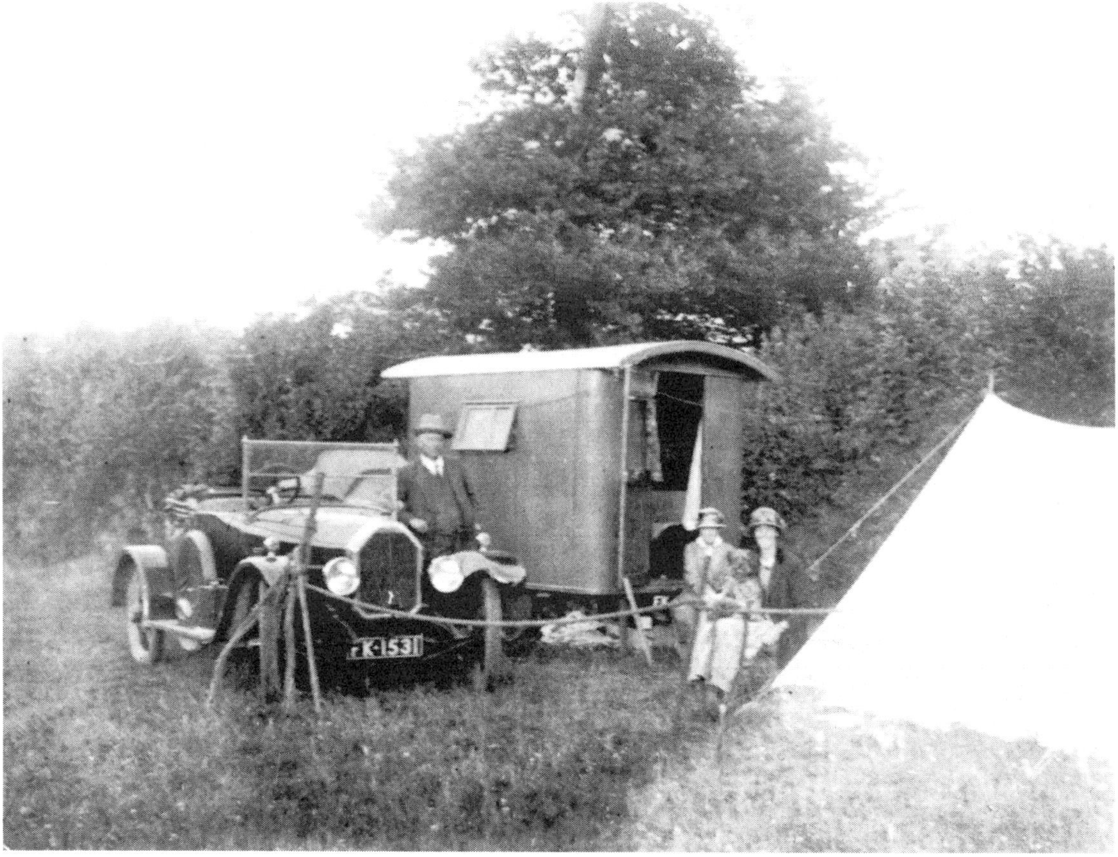

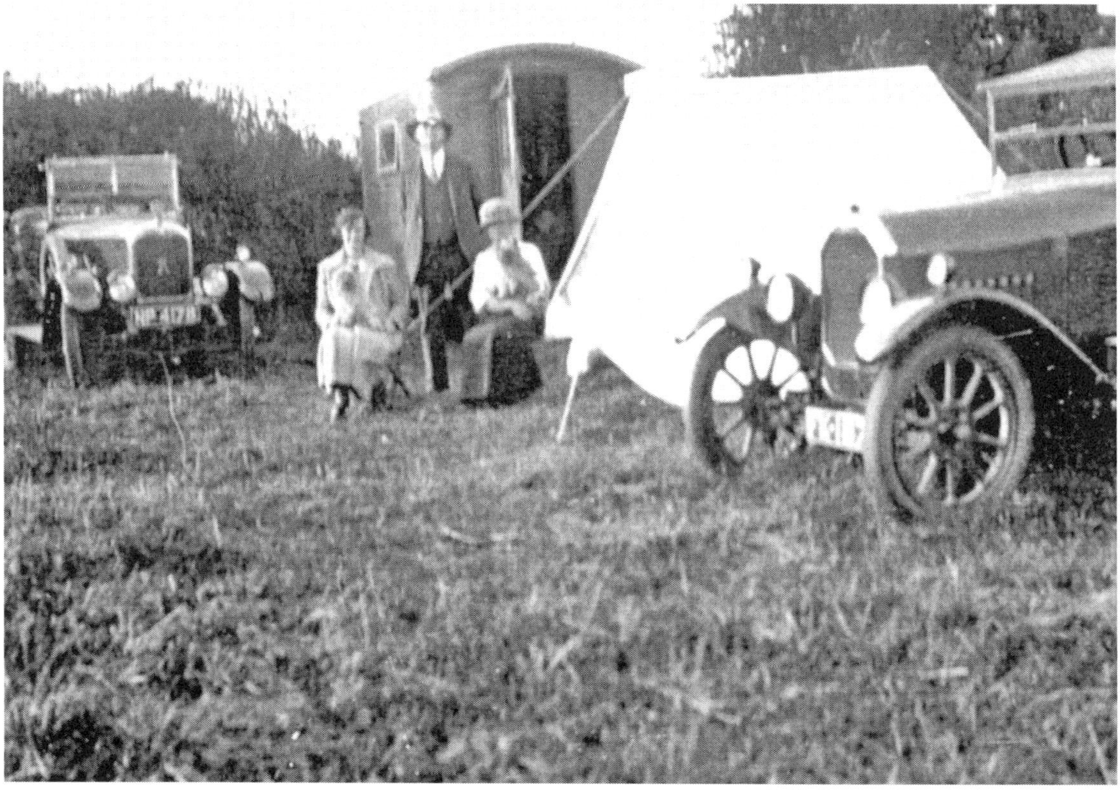

Simple but effective. Here an MG M-type coupé hauls a rather basic homemade caravan. The car has a Herefordshire mark (VJ). (*Pritchard, Hereford*)

*Opposite above:* Despite a growing popularity, the motor-towed caravan was about in far fewer numbers than is the case today, and present-day caravaners would be aghast at the lack of amenities that a small 'van such as the one portrayed here had to offer – little more than somewhere dry in which to eat or sleep in somewhat cramped conditions. The car is a brand-new 1922 Humber 11.4, and as this family changed their car at frequent intervals, it dates the picture fairly accurately. (*The Humber Register*)

*Opposite below:* Even in the mid-1920s, small cars could cope adequately with a light caravan. The cars portrayed here are a Hillman Eleven and a Humber 8/18, both of 1924. The Hillman towed the 'van and the Humber acted as tender car. This family were ardent motoring campers and regularly went far afield like this.

Part of the crowd of sightseers and motorists and their cars who gathered to see the king and the royal family attend Crathie church, near Balmoral, on 20 September 1936.

# 5
# SPORT

Schoolboys, as any schoolmaster knows, are inveterate scribblers and doodlers, and a high proportion of schoolboy doodles since the coming of the mechanical age have been of things mechanical, motorcars included... dreams of the Smith Super Speedster, super-charged, of course, sleek, slim and super-fast, the sportsman's ideal, skidding perilously round this or that course... Brooklands, Le Mans, Monza, Montlhéry... and consigned by schoolmasterly hands to the wastepaper basket in exchange for 200 lines. Sports cars have been defined in as many ways as hordes of minors have dreamed them up in the backs of old exercise books, and it would be a rash man who attempted to define the sports car to suit all tastes.

The popular conception of the 1920s sports car was a rushing, roaring, skimpily-bodied machine totally devoid of comfort or weather protection, and boasting an external exhaust pipe of enormous bore and cacophonous bark; that of the 1930s as a long, low, lengthily-bonneted machine with minimal ground clearance and bedewed with flashy chromium 'goodies' and at least two bonnet straps. Alas, for such conceptions are merely extensions of our schoolboy dreams and deserve the same fate.

Sport is a compound of competition and enjoyment and the photographs in this section reveal how diverse was the type of car that took part. In the earlier part of the inter-war period, events of all kinds were numerous. Brooklands reopened in April 1920 and continued until the outbreak of war in 1939. As had been the case prior to 1914, speed events and hill-climbs could legally be held on the public roads (given a little cooperation from the local police) and seaside resorts ran races on the promenade or on the sand, as at Skegness, Southport or Porthcawl. But spectators were often so foolhardy that, as speeds increased, much anxiety was felt and in some districts, police compliance could not be obtained. The whole matter came to a head at Kop Hill in Bucks in 1925, when a serious accident befell an unfortunate spectator and the RAC imposed a total ban on such events on public roads.

This shifted the emphasis to those few venues where such events could be held on private ground unaffected by the ban. The longest established sprint hill-climb of all, Shelsley Walsh in Worcestershire, famed before the RAC's ban, subsequently gained international status as virtually the only hill-climb venue of any real reputation in Britain. Also, there was an increasing interest in road trials of the tougher, 'off-the-road' kind. Lacking, however, were suitable road circuits for Grand Prix racing or for sports car events such as the classic Le Mans, held on the Continent. True, circuits existed in Ireland, and in the Isle of Man the 'round the town' Mannin Moar and Mannin Beg races in Douglas were the nearest equivalent to the famed Monaco Grand Prix. It was not until 1933 that England had a real road circuit with the opening of Donington Park for motor racing (motorcycle racing had been staged there as from 1931).

The photographs that follow occasionally portray the famous, but most of them instead show some of those thousands of men, and women too, whose names never made the headlines except, perhaps, in their local papers, but without whom the sport as it was could never have flourished.

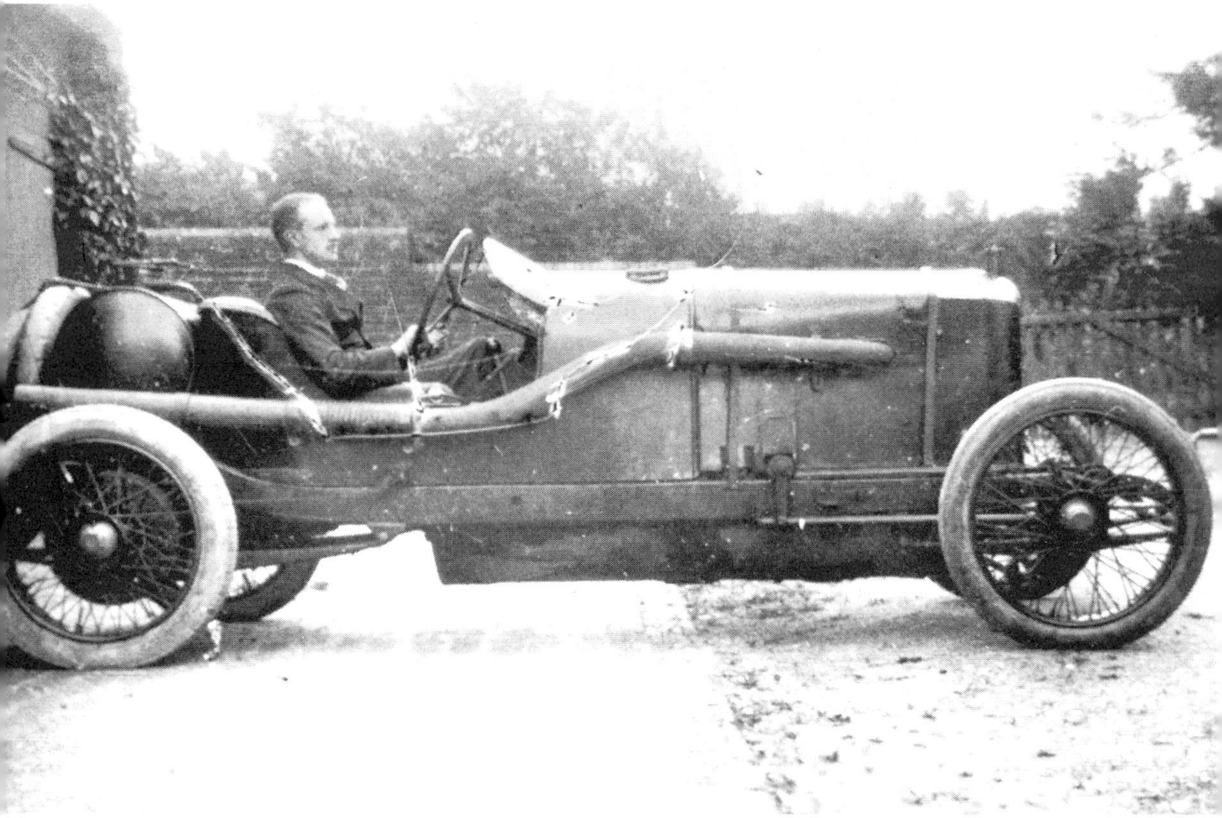

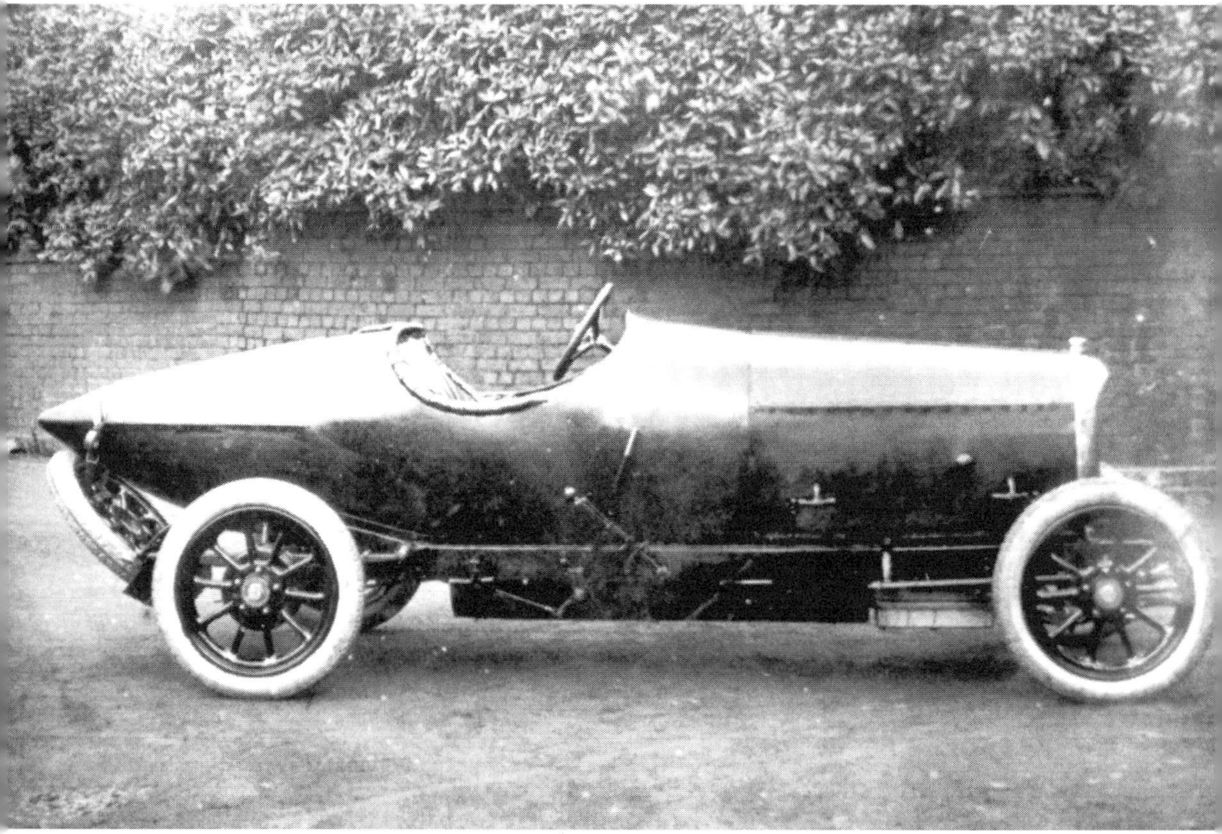

The Junior Car Club held what were termed High Speed Reliability Trials at Brooklands. Members could enjoy themselves in a variety of cars in an event that took in some of the communicating roads within the circuit. In this view, taken on 18 June 1927, Bagshawe's Frazer Nash, which won the event, leads a Ceirano and a very humdrum-looking Austin Seven. (*A. J. Ahern/D. Irvine*)

*Opposite above:* When peace returned, keen amateurs could obtain a fast car relatively cheaply by using outmoded pre-war racing cars. All three of the Humbers raced in the 1914 TT appeared in post-war competition. Here W. G. Barlow, who later raced an Aston Martin and a Bentley, poses in the ex-Tuck Humber of 1914. Barlow first raced this car at Brooklands at the August Bank Holiday meeting, 1920. (*W. G. Barlow/Lord Dudley*)

*Opposite below:* The Hampton was a make that settled into production at Stroud, Gloucestershire, after earlier vicissitudes. Among other things, it became associated with successful climbs of the notorious Nailsworth Ladder nearby. Normally of few sporting pretensions as a make, this example was specially tuned and bodied for use by B. S. Marshall at Brooklands, where it lapped at well over 80 mph in 1922.

The first British GP, Brooklands, Saturday 7 August 1926. Here is a Delage in trouble. The exhaust layout was such that the driver's feet became seriously burnt, a recurrence of a previous malady. Extra louvres have been cut in the scuttle area, but to little effect. This is Robert Sénéchal's car, and it became the winner, averaging 71.61 mph. (*Mrs A. Gripper*)

*Opposite above:* A bevy of officials, led by Sir 'Algy' Guinness, who is accompanied by Lionel Martin, gathers around the Riley driven by C. Paul and J. Phillip during the 500-Miles Race, 24 September 1932. Sir Algernon Guinness was the RAC's chief steward at the time. (*A. B. I. Dick*)

*Opposite below:* The ERA was developed by Peter Berthon, Humphrey Cook and Raymond Mays and inspired and enlivened the British racing scene in the 1930s in road and track races and also, particularly in Mays' hands, at Shelsley Walsh. Here Prince von Leiningen, an early member of the ERA racing team, leads veteran E. R. Hall's MG Magnette away through the fork chicane during the British Empire Trophy Race at Brooklands on 6 July 1935. (*T. A. Roberts*)

73

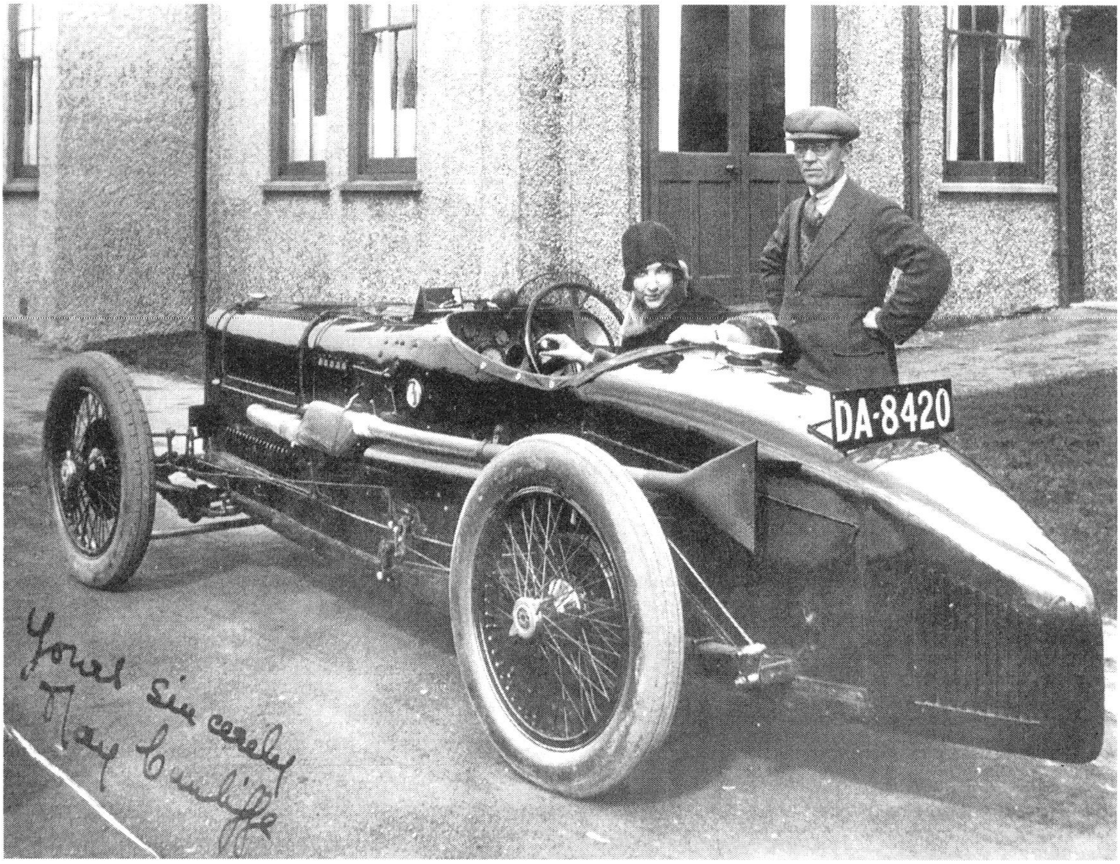
DA-8420
Yours sincerely
May Cunliffe

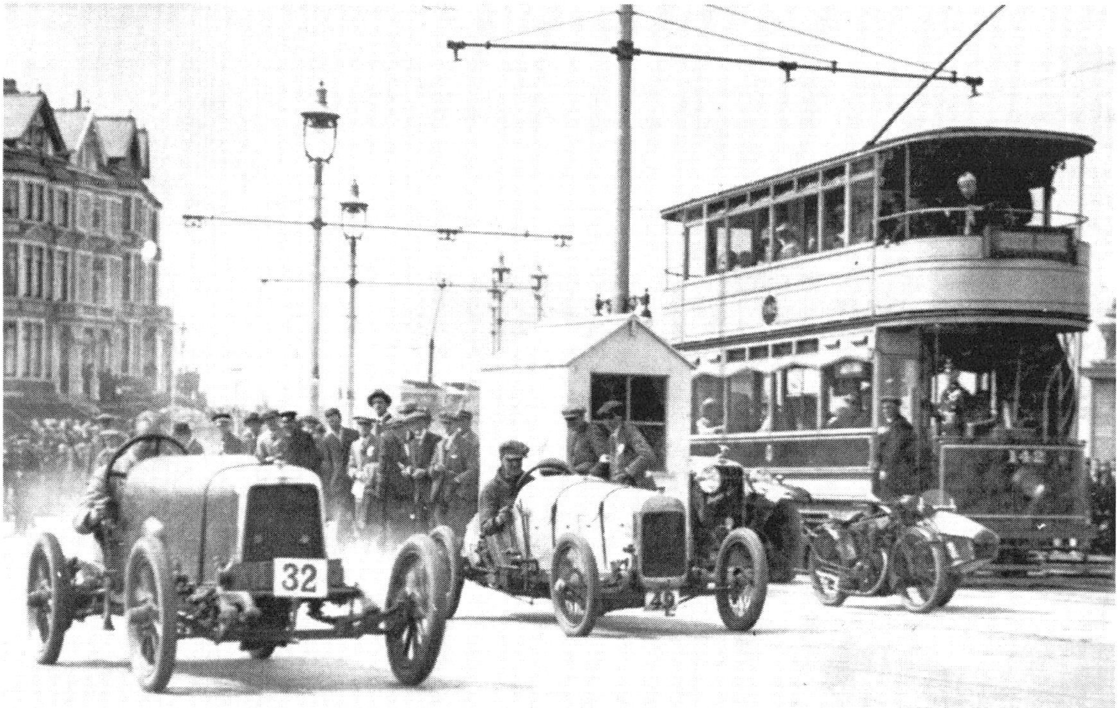
32
142

Long-distance road trials needed considerable organisation, including the use of many 'official cars' to enable officials and marshalls to cover the route. Arrayed here are five official cars and their crews for the ACU Stock Trial of 1925. From left to right they are: I. D. Fell (Riley), the Rev. E. P. Greenhill of the ACU (Palladium), R. Abbott (Clyno), Major A. H. Loughborough of the RAC (Bentley), and Richard Lisle (Star). Ray Abbott added a footnote on the reverse of the photo: 'Every car was capable of over 60 mph on the road.'

*Opposite above:* A magnificent shot of Miss May Cunliffe in the 1924 2-litre Grand Prix Sunbeam, 'equipped' and taxed for the road, be it noted! Miss Cunliffe drove Bentleys and this Sunbeam with considerable success, verve and skill at Shelsley Walsh and at Southport. Beside the car stands Bill Perkins, Sunbeam's chief racing mechanic. (*A. B. I. Dick*)

*Opposite below:* Blackpool Promenade is the scene for this speed contest in which the competitors were sent off in pairs. Here that legendary racing Aston Martin 'Bunny' is slightly quicker off the mark than N. T. Beardsell's racing Hodgson. A delectable Hispano-Suiza hides between the tram and the hut, and the upper-deck passengers in the tram enjoy a grandstand view. (*F. Ellis*)

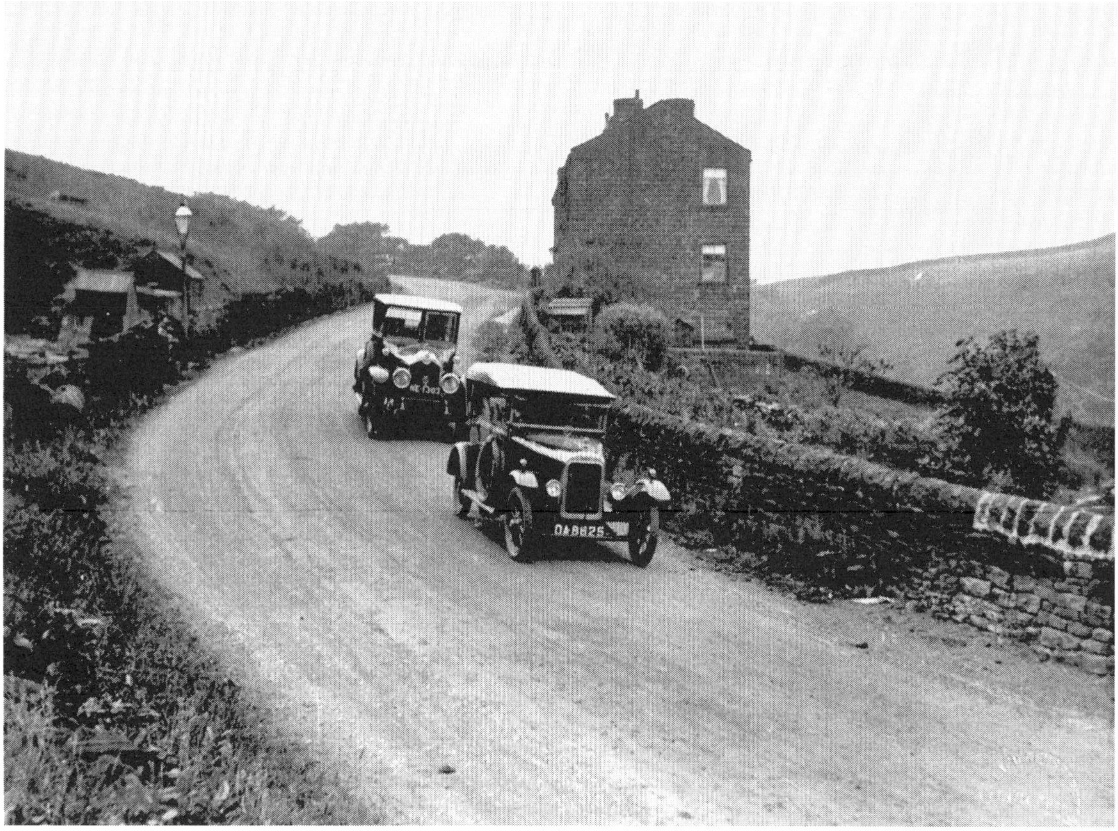

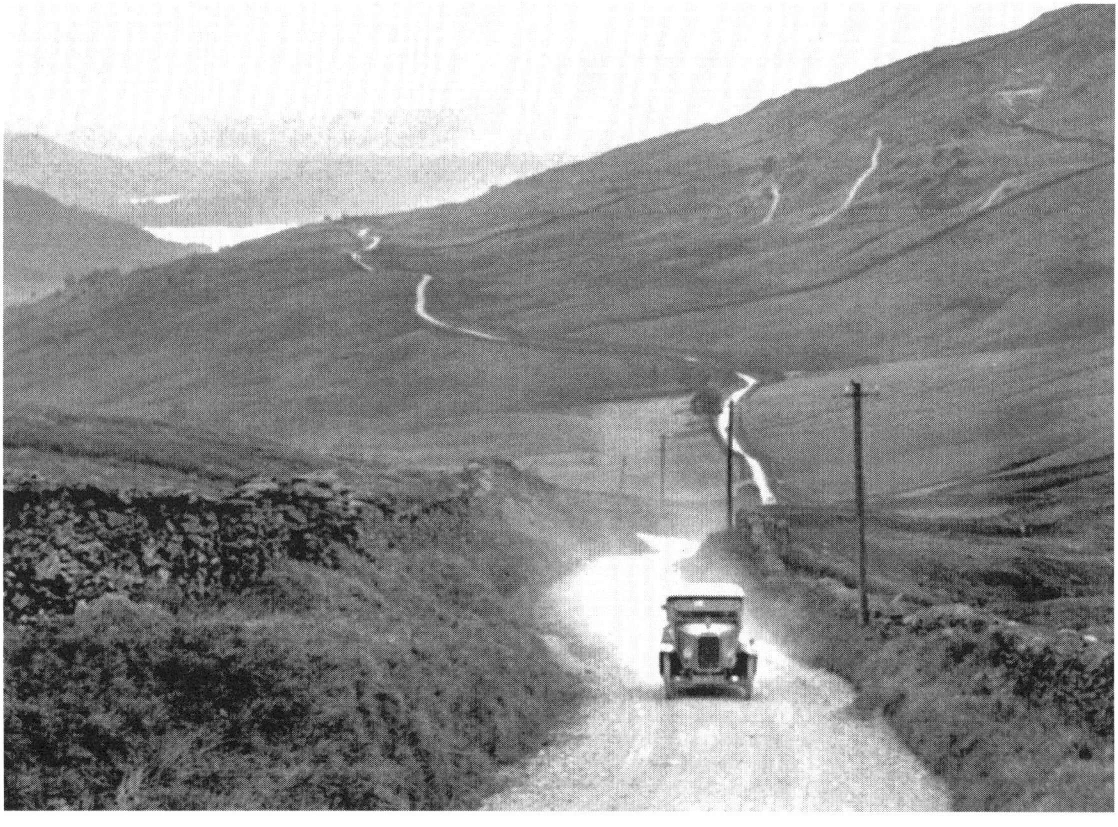

Abbott's Clyno on Mytholm Steeps in the same event. He had the third fastest mile out of ninety-six entries.

*Opposite, above and below:* Two competitors in the 1925 £1,000 Trial tackle Kirkstone Pass. They are a Crossley and A. R Abbott's Clyno. Successes gained by any particular make in such trials were widely advertised by the manufacturers and were a valuable aid to sales promotion. In later years, as the trials themselves and the cars that entered for them became more specialised, the public as a whole became less influenced by such performances.

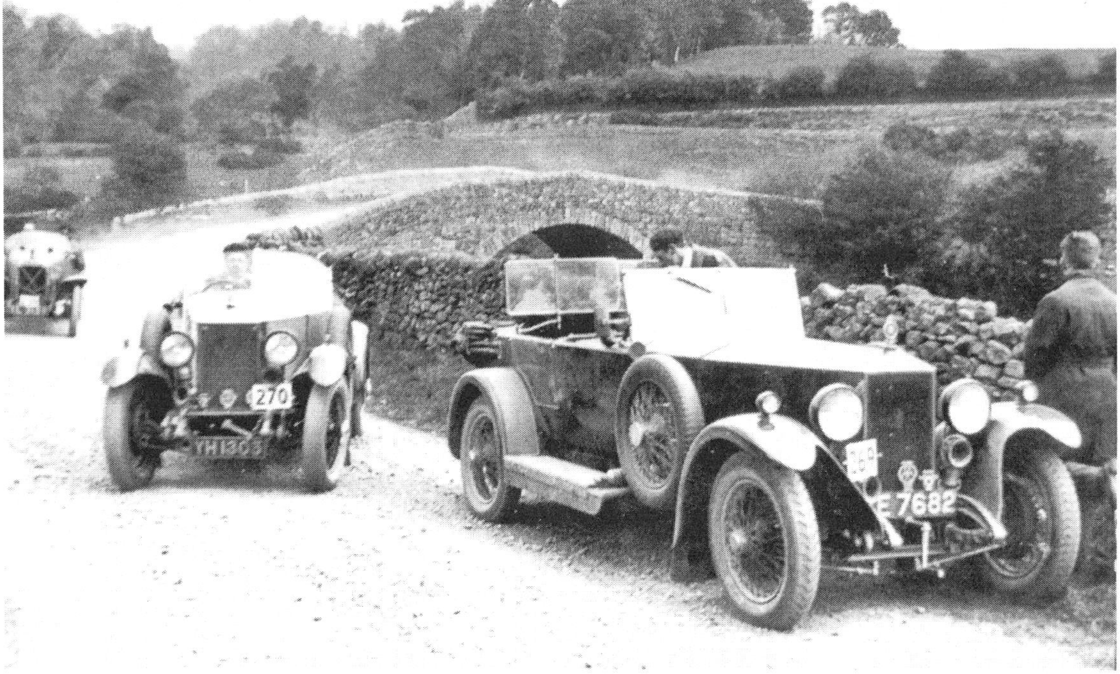
270
YH1303
E 7682

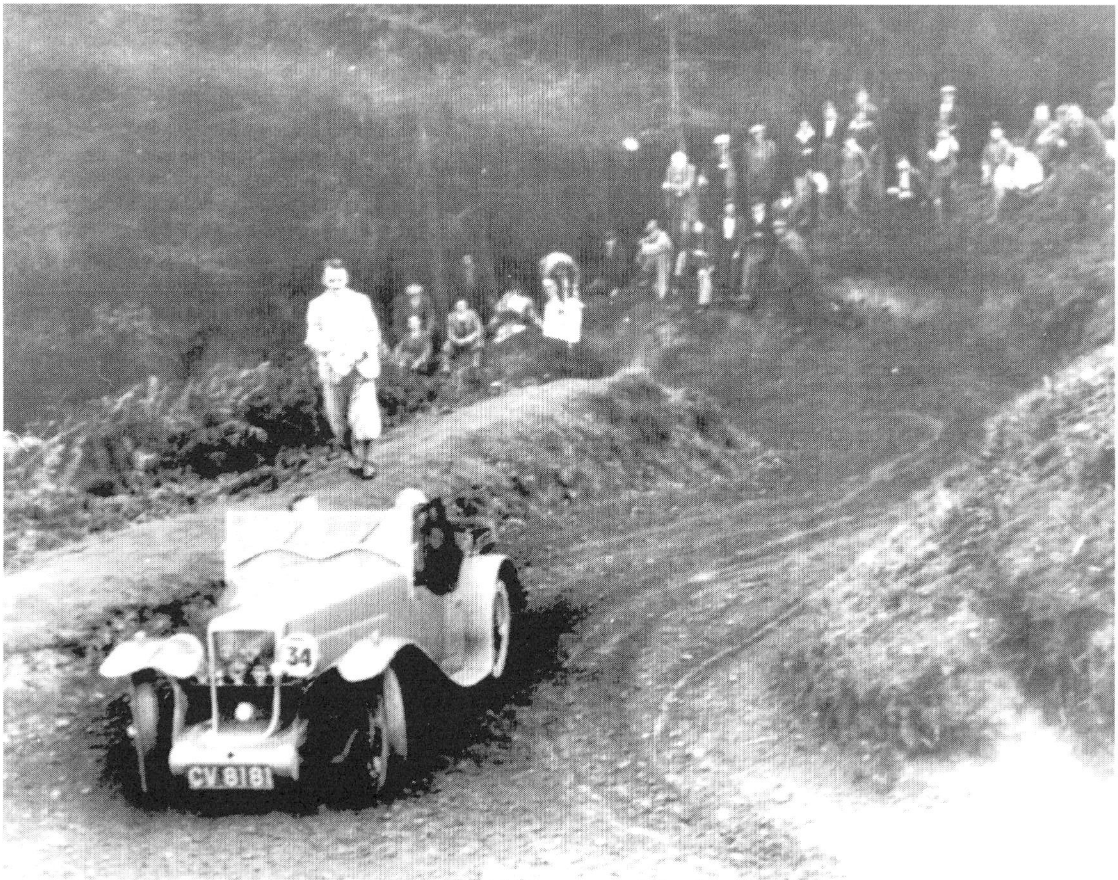
34
CV 8181

MG Midgets enjoyed many competition successes from the time of their introduction, in road, track and trials events. This P-type Midget carries twin 'knobbly'-tyred spare wheels and displays the fruits of its labours proudly on the bonnet.

*Opposite above:* Two Invictas are here taking part in an MCC London-Edinburgh trial in 1928. (*J. Ahern/D. Irvine*)

*Opposite below:* Cornishman W. P. Uglow, a well-known trials expert of the 1930s, takes his March Special Hillman Aero-Minx up Doverhay in an MCC Trial of the time.

Both Oxford and Cambridge universities sported active motoring clubs in which keen undergraduates made up for the restrictions on motoring activities imposed by the university authorities. Here, at the CUAC's one-day event of the 1921 season, a sports Morris Cowley and a Rhode line up for the fun. (*W. H. Summers*)

*Opposite above:* Humphrey Cook's famous Vauxhall 30/98 was often in the award lists at 1920s events. The car was nicknamed 'Rouge et Noir'. (*S. Hall*)

*Opposite below:* At the many speed events going on almost every weekend in 'the season', the atmosphere was friendly and, until the disaster at Kop Hill early in 1925, restrictions were few. Already a name to reckon with in the early 1920s, Raymond Mays was to become one of the aces of speed hill-climbs. He is seen here with his famous Bugatti 'Cordon Rouge' at Madresfield in 1922. (*R. Mays*)

81

Swansong for a dying make. E. R. Hall, veteran of many Shelsleys, takes the 2,362 cc Cozette-supercharged Arrol-Aster up the hill in September 1929. Unlikely entries of these cars in the Ulster Tourist Trophy (the race number 61 still visible on the body side in this shot) and the Alpine Trial brought some publicity, but this was the last fling for the unfortunate marriage between Scotland and Wembley that united Arrol-Johnston with Aster, the firm going into liquidation in that same year, 1929. (*Midland AC*)

*Opposite above:* Being on private ground, Shelsley Walsh was unaffected by the 1925 ban and gained immeasurably in popularity and stature, achieving international status by 1930. In 1931 Spain sent two Nacional Pescaras to the hill, driven by Zanelli and Tort. They failed either to take FTD or the record. This view shows Zanelli's car at the top of the hill. On the left is Earl Howe's ex-Caracciola Mercedes-Benz. (*Midland AC*)

*Opposite below:* Malcolm Campbell was a household name between the wars and here, in May 1935, eagerly watched as usual, he comes up to the start line at Shelsley Walsh in his sleek Sunbeam. But Mays' 39.6 seconds won the day and the record. (*Midland AC*)

83

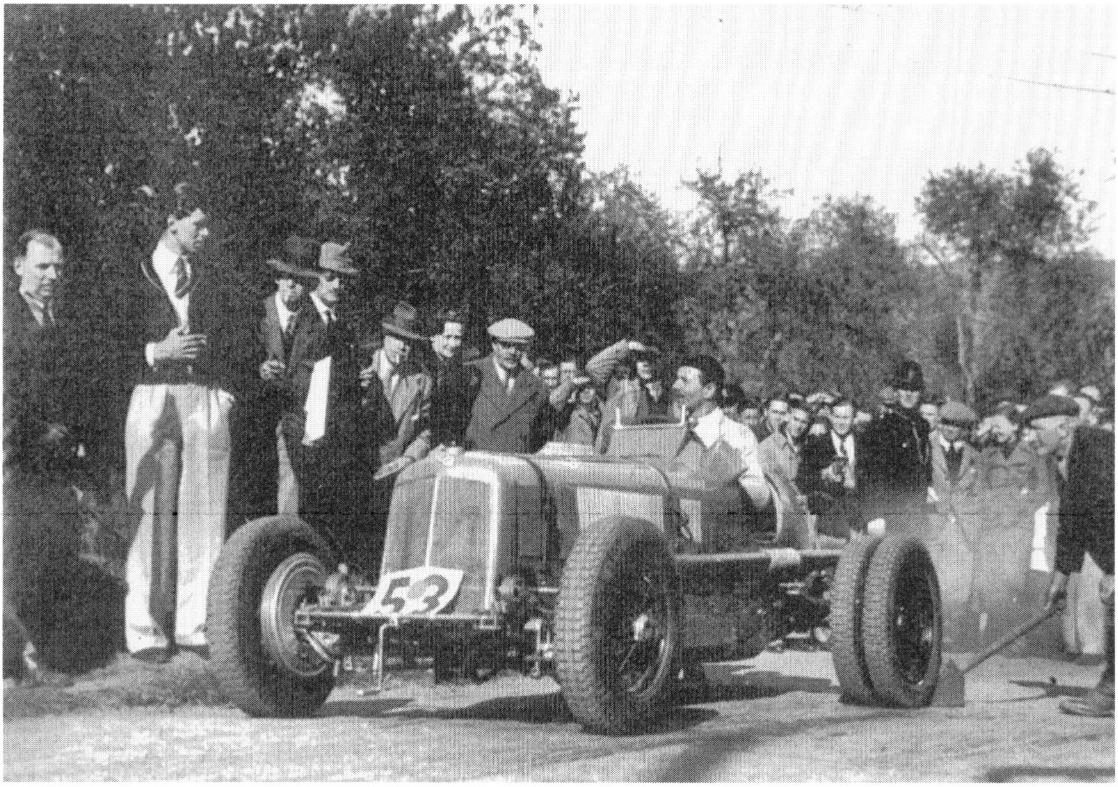
53

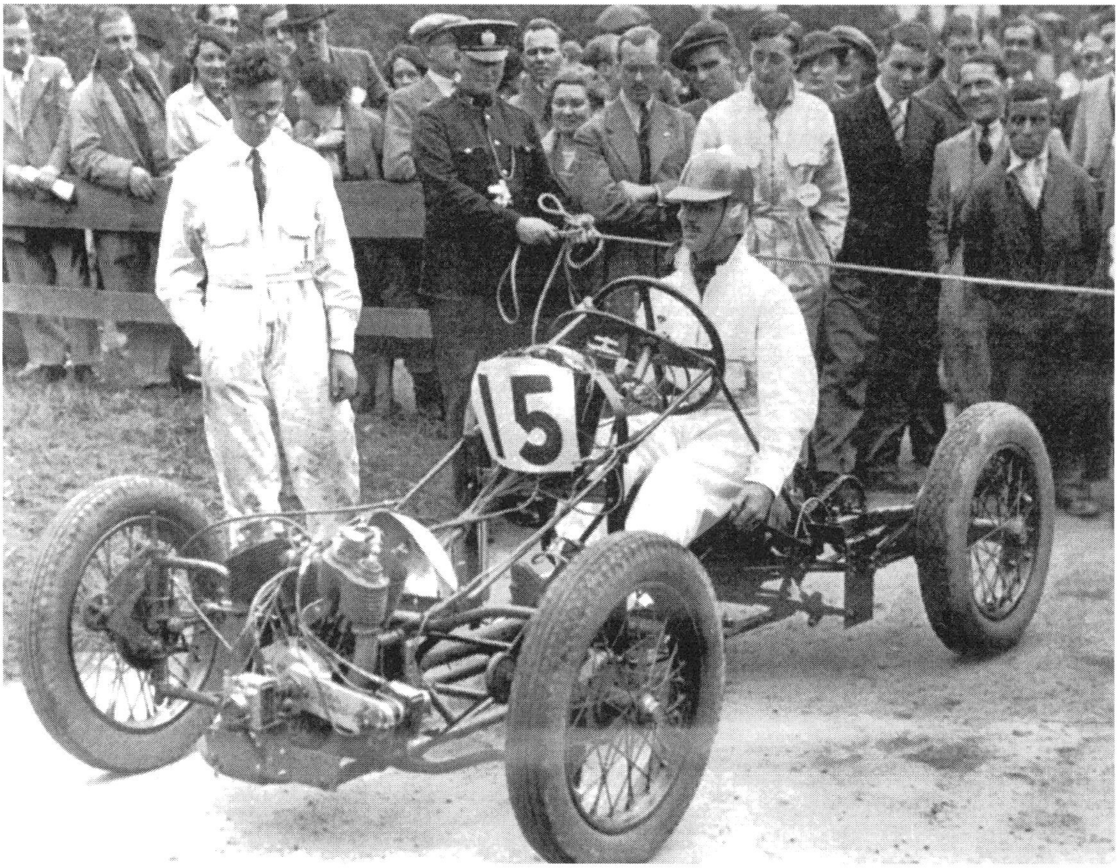
5

A. F. P. Fane brings his Frazer Nash-BMW through the Esses at Shelsley Walsh at the June 1936 meeting, watched by a dense crowd. These cars offered a new concept of sports car motoring that was only to be fully developed after the Second World War. (*Midland AC*)

*Oppsite above:* A historic moment! Raymond Mays is about to make the first under-40 seconds climb of Shelsley Walsh with his ERA in May 1935. Expectancy is written clear on every face and they were not to be disappointed. (*Midland AC*)

*Opposite below:* Shelsley Walsh engendered a whole tribe of 'Shelsley Specials', often amateur-built but all inspired by the one idea of getting up the hill as fast as possible. As in this example, many of them dispensed power and noise in unashamed nakedness. This is the 'Joystick Special' about to go into action at the September 1935 event. (*Midland AC*)

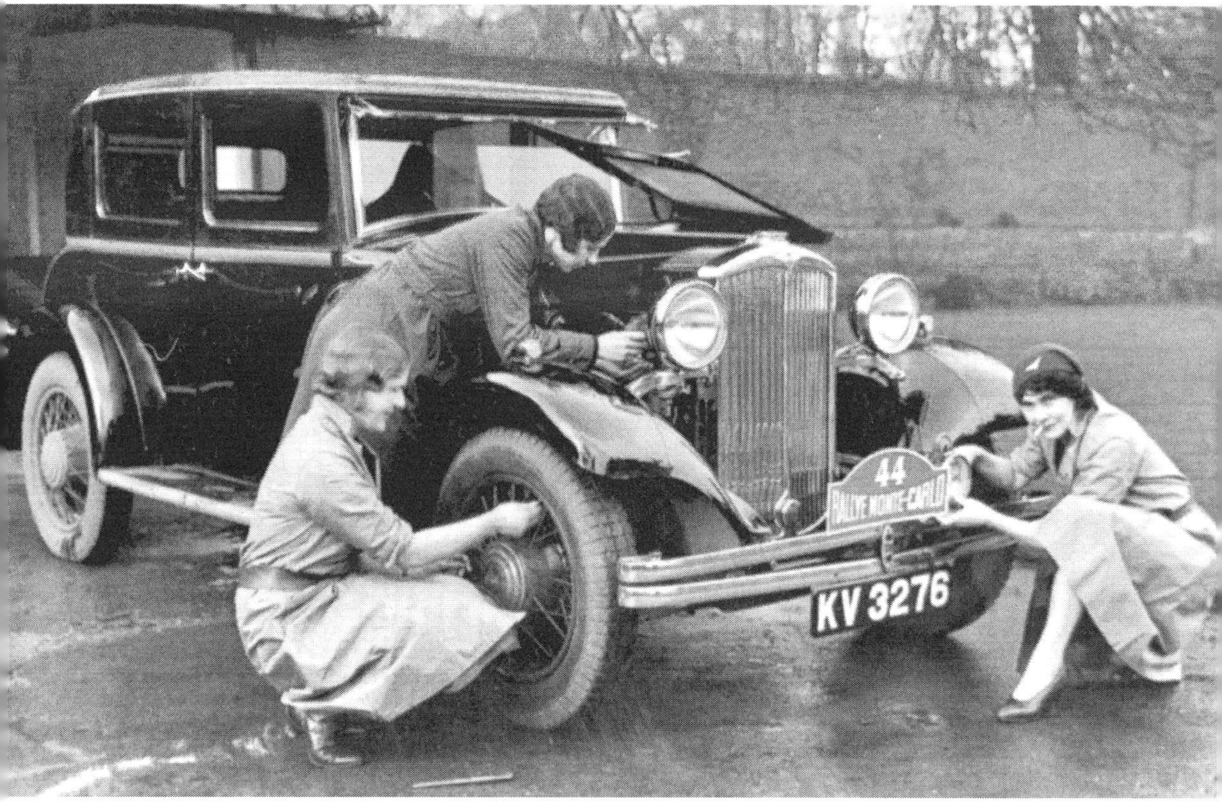
44
RALLYE MONTE-CARLO
KV 3276

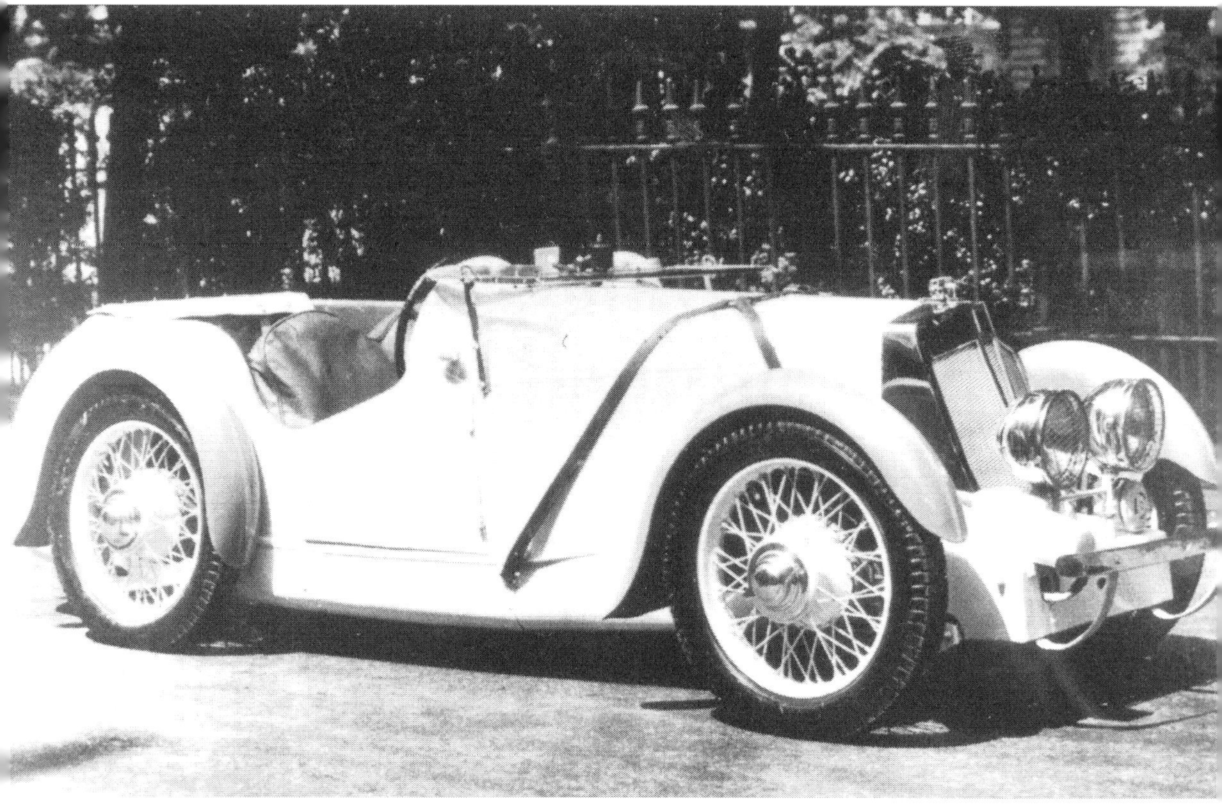

The Hon. Mrs Victor Bruce at the wheel of the Hillman Straight-8 'Segrave' sports saloon in which she entered a Monte Carlo Rally, starting from Lapland. Some years earlier, her husband had been the first Britisher in a British car, an AC, to win the event. (*J. Irvine*)

*Opposite above:* An all-female crew, this time for the Monte Carlo Rally of 1933. This Hillman 'Wizard' was driven from John O'Groats by Barbara Marshall, Agnes Gripper and Katherine Martin, all experienced competition drivers. They had many minor adventures en route, including an involuntary fire, but reached Monte Carlo successfully and were awarded the Ladies' Cup. (*John Martin*)

*Opposite below:* This ultra-low-slung sports car of the 1930s is a Vale Special 'Tourette', which contrived to cram a four-seater body within its limited wheelbase. These small sports cars were the very antithesis of what the vintage purists liked, but nevertheless they had many successes in races and other competitions. (*D. Cox*)

Land-speed-record holders were ever-popular heroes and every schoolboy could recite the exploits of Sir Malcolm Campbell and his 'Bluebirds'. Hidden beneath this ingenious mock-up is a very prosaic Citroën. The date is probably between February 1931 and February 1932, but even so, somebody got their sums wrong; Campbell's speeds on both occasions differed from the legend on the tail. (*Watson's Motor Works*)

When the Germans brought Mercedes-Benz and Auto-Union racers to Donington Park in the late 1930s, their superiority was marked. Here, Berndt Rosemeyer's Auto-Union shows a fine line in 1938.

# 6
# SERVING THE PUBLIC

Almost from the earliest days of the motor age, the motor vehicle, with substantial assistance from the steam vehicle for heavy work, was pressed into the service of the public, and never was its worth better indicated than in the 1914–18 war. The developments of the inter-war years were significant and far-reaching, primarily in that for the first time, road transport in the service of the public became a serious challenge to the long-held supremacy of the railways, instead of being ancillary to them.

Improved techniques of tyre construction enabled heavy vehicles to use pneumatics instead of the solids hitherto almost universal – a development first favoured for passenger vehicles and later spreading to goods vehicles as well. The introduction and spread of the diesel-engined vehicle and discriminatory tax legislation forced the steamer, popular for the heaviest jobs, off the roads, and the articulated lorry, introduced in six-wheeler form to Britain by Scammell in 1920, led the way to higher payloads.

During the 1920s, small country bus services proliferated, many of them started by ex-servicemen, first with wartime vehicles adapted for the job and later with purpose-built vehicles. What a valuable, personal and friendly service they performed. The buses and staff were known and often nicknamed by all. They were accommodating and adaptive as no urban bus service could ever be. Even the railways themselves ran feeder services, seemingly unaware of the threat the bus services posed to their own existence.

Charabancs – high, unwieldy and crammed with usually noisy pleasure-seekers, or empty and simmering in the afternoon seaside sun, awaiting a mystery tour – were popular in holiday areas, but by the late 1920s they had largely given place to more sophisticated long-distance coaches, which offered cheaper fares than the railways. In smaller vehicles and for shorter journeys, the variety was as great as the purposes to which the vehicles were put. Even battery-electric transport survived in urban areas for the whole of the period under review; for specific purposes such as house-to-house milk delivery, their use increased.

As for the hire car or taxi (London's taxis being creatures apart), almost every village could boast at least one by the 1930s, and what a splendidly varied assortment of ageing automobiles most of them were, ranging from the humdrum to the faded gentility of former exotica, eking out their days in frowsty but dignified shabbiness.

One of the most successful of steam wagon makers was Sentinel of Shrewsbury, and this is one of its Super-Sentinels, new on 17 March 1924. Many steam operators perpetuated the tradition of elaborate painting and lining out; the livery of this example was bright scarlet with black chassis and running gear, and the gold lettering was shaded with blue. This wagon carries its fleet number, 16. Most of the fleet were also steamers. (*S. Llewellyn*)

South Monmouthshire supported much industry and this late Sentinel S8 wagon – with shaft drive and on pneumatic tyres and with electric lighting – is not easily distinguishable as a steamer, apart from the small protrusion of the chimney from the cab roof. W. Whiting was yet another Abergavenny haulage contractor.

Steam had by no means lost the battle for the really heavy jobs until it was forced out by partisan legislation and the spreading use of the diesel lorry in the 1930s. These three are the products of Mann's Patent Steam Cart & Wagon Co. of Leeds, and show every sign of leading a hard life. (*National Library of Wales*)

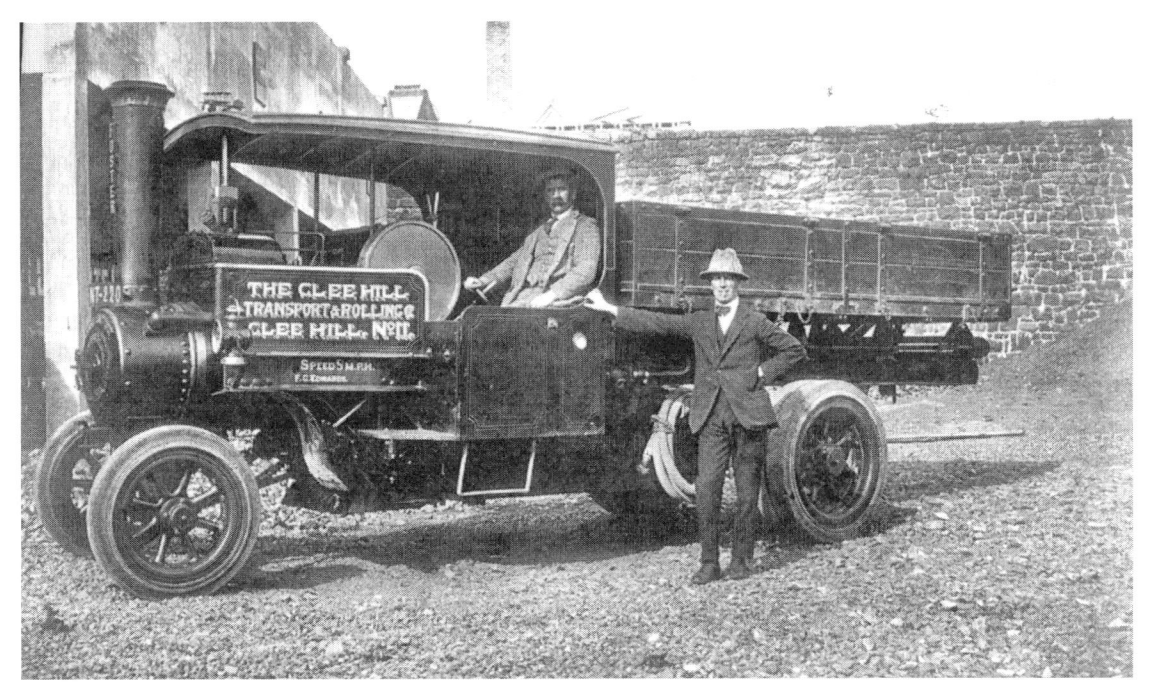

This Foster Overtype steam wagon with a Shropshire registration was one of a fleet of similar wagons engaged in the transport of Dhustone road-surfacing material from the Clee Hill quarries. Note the elaborate and decorative signwriting, and, remarkably, the model biplane affixed to the cabin roof. Perhaps the wagon was the flyer of the fleet. (*Ludlow Library*)

BX-1918

THE CENTRAL
GARAGE
DODGE
MOTOR
SALES AND
Mobiloil
Standard

A Sentinel steamer at work as a tar sprayer when owned by W. & J. Glossop of West Yorkshire. It was new on 23 December 1930. (*A. R. Thomas*)

*Opposite above:* It's new, it's theirs, and they're proud of it. The Model T Ford, the 'Tin Lizzie', was a widely-used and long-suffering vehicle that could still be a willing worker at a ripe old age. Even the signwriter has enjoyed himself. (*National Library of Wales*)

*Opposite below:* The Central Garage in Kington, Herefordshire, proclaims itself a Dodge agent. Here we see a new Dodge taxi; a white-coated chauffeur stands ready for hire. (*Kington Library*)

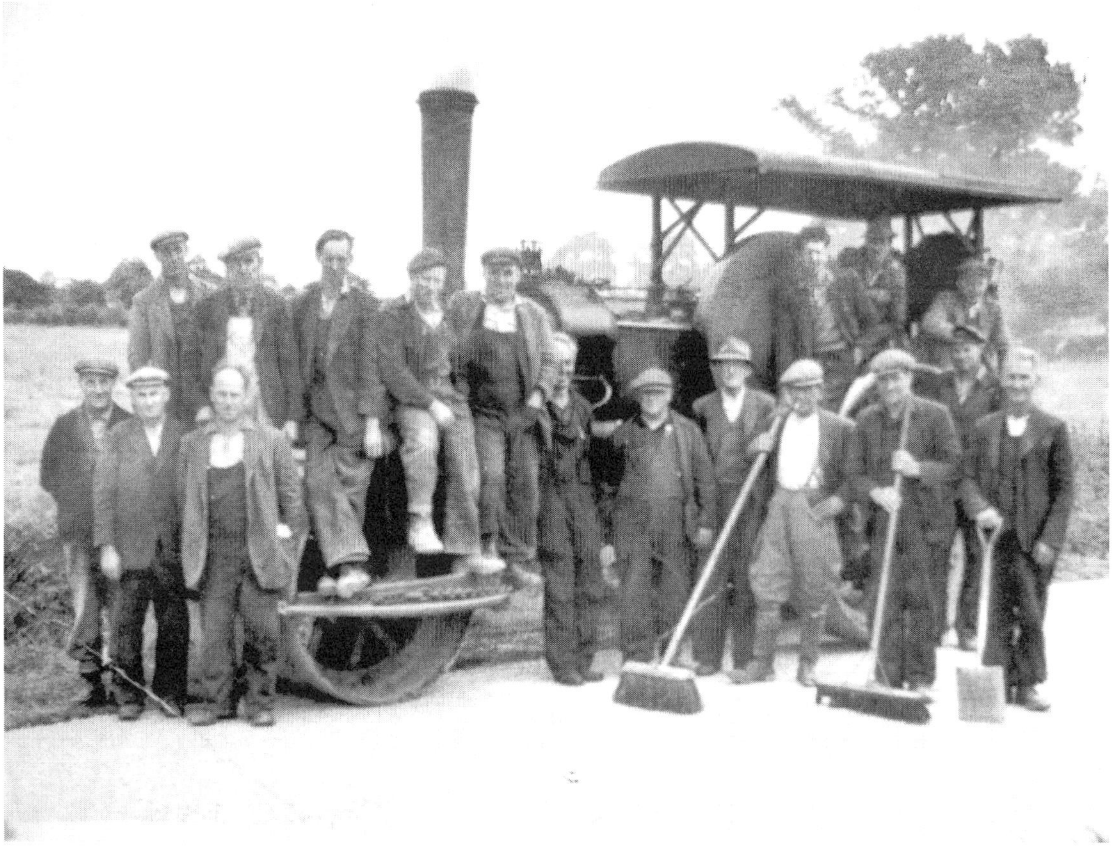

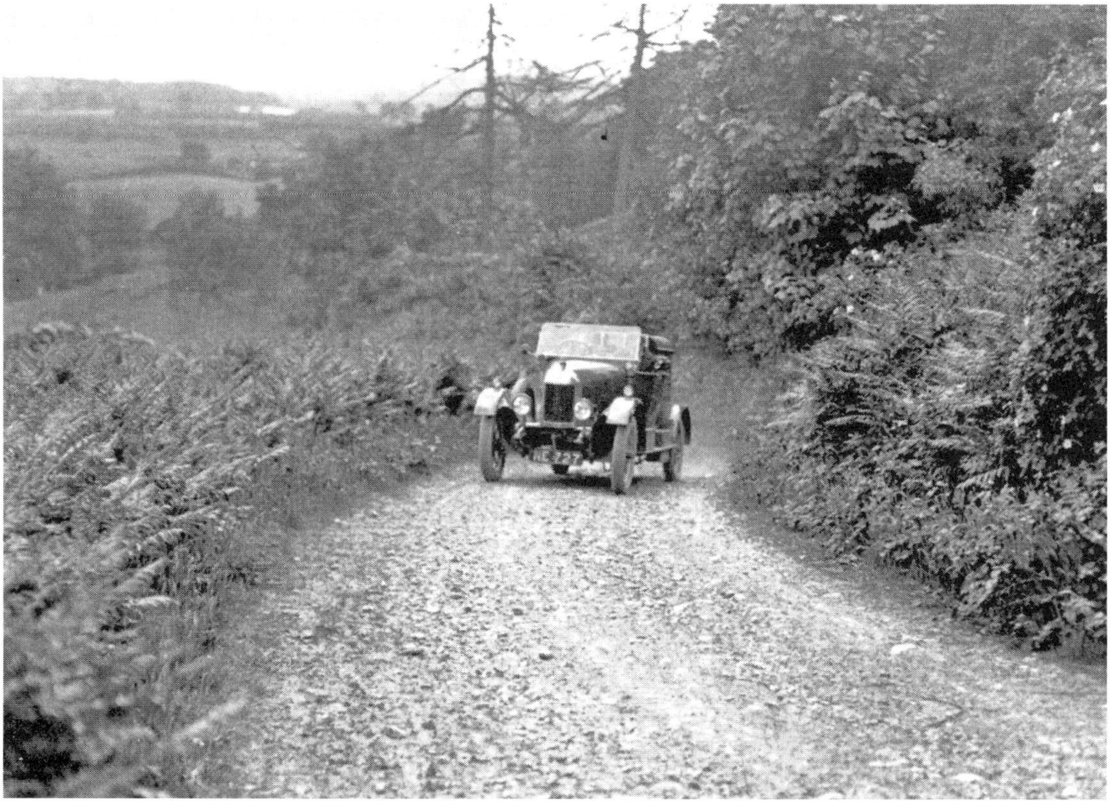

Wireless was all the rage when this 'Bullnose' Morris advertised its owner's wares. One can just imagine the magic sounds of 2LO emerging from that vast loudspeaker, but it must have swallowed some miles per hour in drag.

*Opposite above:* Road repairs were always an essential public service. Here is an Aveling & Porter roller, registered NT 8947, with its crew at work. This roller spent all its life with the Shropshire County Council. (*A. R. Thomas*)

*Opposite below:* A 'Bullnose' Morris with a travellers' brougham body traverses a lonely road while about its daily workload.

CARS FOR HIRE
Proprietor
E. RAYNER
CROUCH END
STATION
GARAGE
LU 4121

BELLE VUE HOTEL

This Daimler charabanc is proving a popular attraction in Leominster, Herefordshire.

*Opposite above:* A Fiat and two Sunbeams in use as hire cars pose with their drivers in 1925. Not all hire cars were maintained so immaculately, but to keep them so must have been an excellent advertisement for Mr Rayner's business.

*Opposite below:* 'Stand for Licensed Taxis Only' proclaims the notice, and its guardian has certainly been a licensed taxi for very many years. Such Edwardian relics could be found plying for hire well into the 1930s, their engines becoming wheezier and their upholstery mustier as the years went by. (*Norman May's Studio Ltd*)

Ludlow was justifiably proud of its new Leyland fire engine, registered in Shropshire as BAW 475. (*Ludlow Museum*)

*Opposite above:* This Fowler pulls an exceptional load, and thus provides the contractor with an advertisement worth recording. (*A. R. Thomas*)

*Opposite below:* If it were not for the small protrusion of the chimney above the cab roof, it would be hard to recognise this handsome Foden wagon as a steamer. (*Cheshire Record Office*)

FROM **F. C. FLOWER**, Heavy Haulage Contractor, **LEDBURY.**

**KRUPP STEEL TUBE.**—Nett Weight 26 Tons.

J. L. PENFOLD, BARNHAM, SUSSEX.

PHONE EASTERGATE 118

*Above:* Garner formed an unlikely alliance with Sentinel of Shrewsbury and produced the Garner-Sentinel, which was diesel-powered. Its appearance is still, however, very much like that of the steamers.

*Left:* The driver extends an invitation to step aboard this Newton Abbott charabanc in the 1920s.

This Worcester trader uses a Morris Oxford saloon with trailer for his business. It was also used, as here, as a public address system at events. (*H. A. Bullock*)

Standard Sentinel wagon No. 2620 was new to Greenlands Ltd, Hereford, in 1920. It was sold to William Bengry, Kingsland, and was last licensed in April 1934, registration number AW 5740. (*T. Thomas*)

A scruffy Sentinel S4 shaft-driven wagon used by Bulmers of Hereford, the renowned cider makers. Registered with the Shropshire mark UJ 3113, this wagon was new on 1 May 1934. Said to have covered some 500,000 miles with Bulmers, it ended its days in Argentina – at a Patagonia Rio Tinto mine. (*J. L. Thomas*)

# 7
# REPAIRS & REPLENISHMENTS

Cars breed garages, garages breed cars... a chicken and egg situation perhaps? A more noteworthy feature of the inter-war period than the increase in the numbers of cars and garages, which was only to be expected, was the changing relationship between the two, as compared with the earlier years of motoring. Prior to 1914, garages, large or small, were almost invariably part and parcel of a settlement – a town or a city, or even a village. In the next two decades, a change became increasingly apparent, caused by two entirely separate developments. The first was the adoption of the petrol pump in place of the hitherto universal can; the second was the building of arterial roads expressly for motor traffic rather than Chesterton's 'rolling English road' of earlier times. The motorcar's own contribution was the mobility it gave.

These new factors gave rise to the filling-station, made possible by the petrol pumps and required at intervals along the lengthy new arterial roads well away from existing settlements, reached by the operator by motor as easily as by his customers. It was not a garage in the strict sense; it dispensed fuel and lubricating oils essentially, and often tyres and accessories as well. It did not buy, sell or repair cars, though in many cases it sold sweets, cigarettes and sundries. It did its job with varying efficiency, but too often it became an eyesore, smothered with garish advertisements, untidy, a ready depository for the motorists' litter and the owners' mechanical junk.

Sometimes it blossomed, if that is the word, into that other phenomenon of the time, the roadhouse, a forerunner of the motel, a product of a pleasure-seeking age that largely relied on the motor for its pleasures, and all too often as brash and tasteless in its conception and execution as in its service to its customers. However, it apparently fulfilled their needs.

Unfortunately, the public service sector was often no less an offender in the part it played in the spoiling of the countryside. The architectural standards of the best of Victorian railway stations were not those of the bus and coach operators, which tended to be utilitarian eyesores, all too frequently tucked away (perhaps mercifully) behind ugly backs of existing buildings, or wide open spaces like overgrown car parks, draughty, exposed to the elements, and a paradise for litter.

Major repairs required here. Lionel Martin, founder of the Aston Martin firm, loved speed. He was towing this engineless racer and rashly succumbed to a speed duel with the sorry result portrayed. The car was repaired. (*Addis/Henley Collection*)

Those with an eye for the ephemera of motoring will find much to satisfy them in the early signs and the Pratts' petrol pump at the kerbside. The nearer of the two cars is an early Tipo 501 Fiat, one of the most popular of that company's offerings. (*Kington Library*)

Mass production (copied from America) made cheap transport more widely available but planted the seeds of traffic jams and overcrowding. The coming of the petrol pump brought a mushroom growth of filling-stations; these newly-opened premises dispensed 'R.O.P.' – Russian Oil Products. (*M. Dowty*)

Photographed here is Handel Davies' Brooklands Garage, Garnant, in around 1925. The vehicles are, from left to right, a Jowett, a James motorcycle, an AJS motorcycle, a 1924 Sunbeam motorcycle, an AJS motorcycle and a Raleigh motorcycle. Handel himself stands in the centre of the picture. (*Lynn Hughes*)

A delivery of Overland cars and a light van, together with a solitary 14-hp Crossley tourer (fifth from the left) to a small town garage, *c.* 1924. American cars were popular in outlying districts on account of their lack of complication and relatively powerful but 'woolly' engines. The standard sedan (far left) contrasts strongly with the English-bodied landaulette next to it. (*Library of Wales*)

Many such filling stations rapidly became disfigured by a rash of indiscriminate advertisements and signs, adding what might be termed an unsightly chapter to motoring architecture. This example is less untidy than many.

*Above:* A Bayliss-Thomas exchanges its old beaded-edge tyres with their narrow section for a set of balloon tyres for added comfort...

*Right:* ...and the job is completed with the new Michelin 'Confort' low-pressure tyres in place. The high-pressure tyres are piled on the left.

This Vauxhall 30/98 often toured abroad. On such tours it was advisable to be mechanically capable, since continental mechanics were largely unfamiliar with British cars. (*G. S. Boston*)

Although this early four-cylinder Brecia Bugatti hasn't the classic beauty of Bugatti's later eight-cylinder engines, it is still unmistakably a Bugatti design. Whether its owner is merely admiring it or is puzzled by a mechanical malady is unclear.

Edward Mills bends over the bonnet of Violette Cordery's Invicta during a record attempt at Monza. (*E. Mills*)

Broad Street, Worcester, on a sunny morning. The Austin 7 is parked rather far out from the kerb, perhaps to allow the young girl to step out onto the pavement. The former tramlines have now all gone. (*W. W. Dowty*)

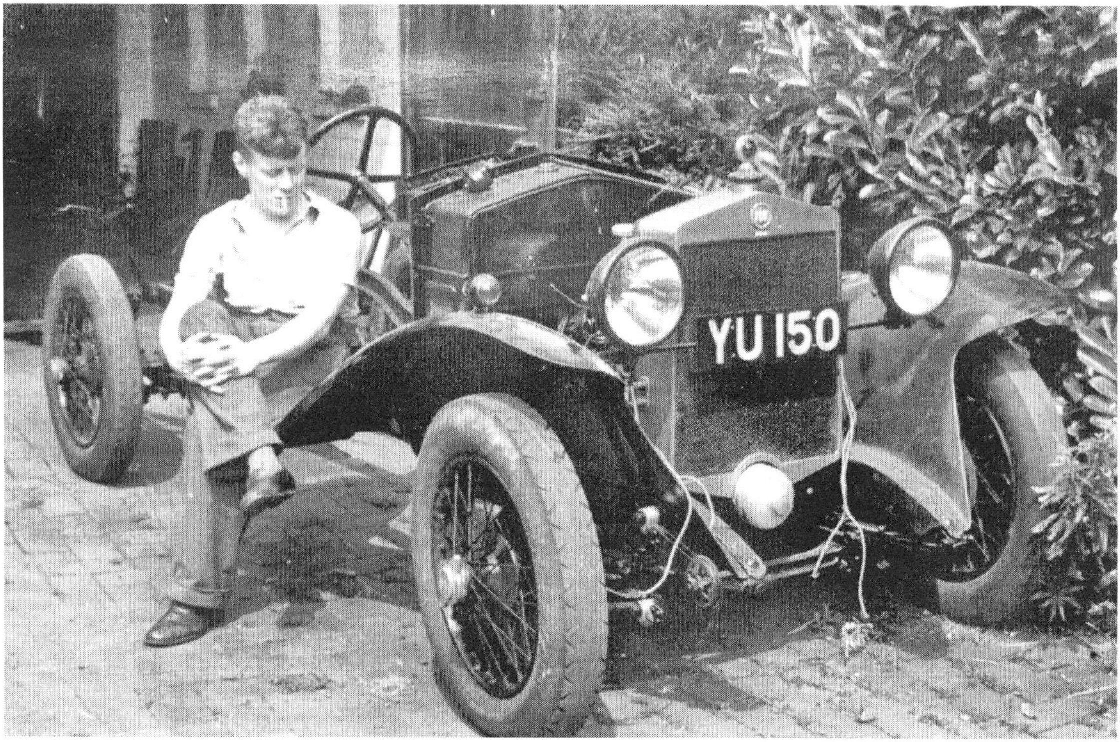
YU 150

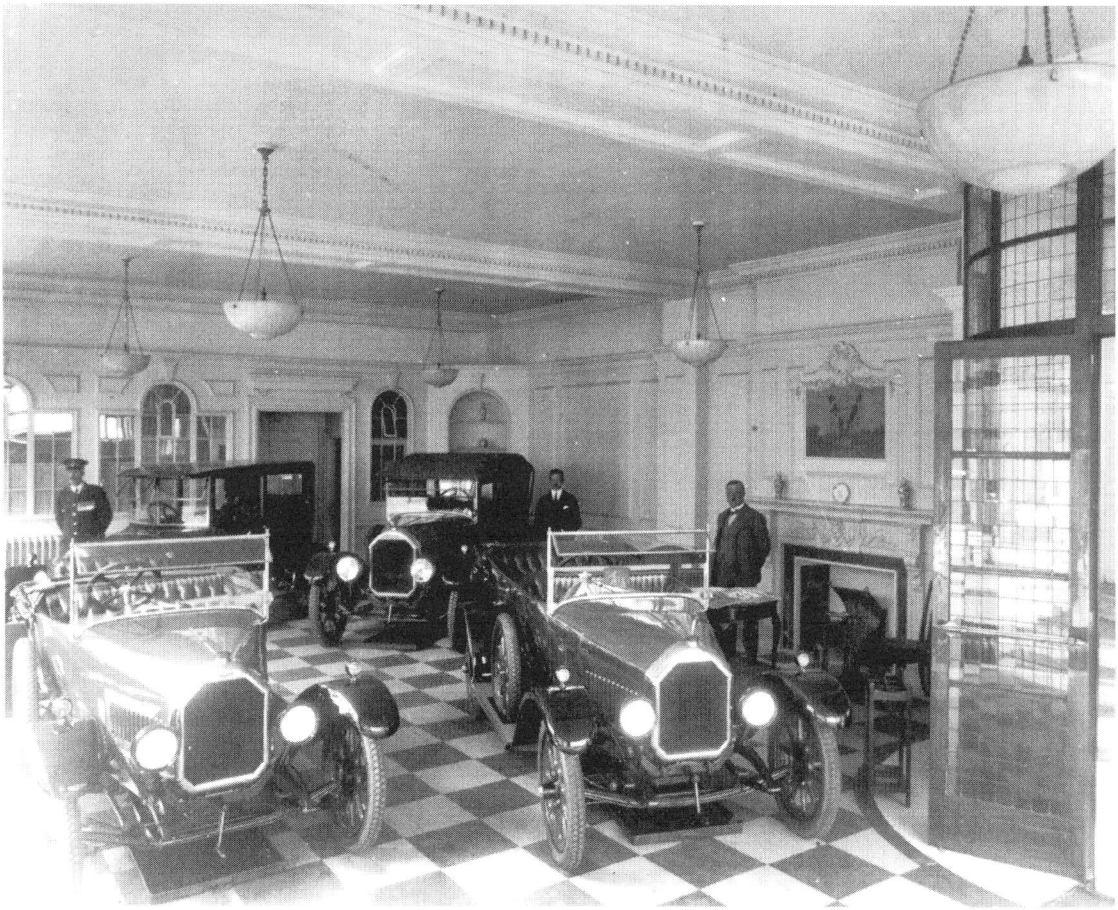

Here in the Finishing Stop a range of 11.4-hp and 15.9-hp Humbers may be seen in various stages of completion. A far cry from present-day robots!

*Opposite above:* Rather more of a rebuild than casual maintenance. Here we see Charlie Sgonina, the 'Welsh Wizard' motorcycling ace, survey the prospect of a lot of work on his sporting Fiat 509S. (*Mrs C. Sgonina*)

*Opposite below:* Showrooms and offices in the metropolis were key to linking manufacturer and customer. This is Humber's Holborn Viaduct Showroom in 1922.

The aircraft add an unusual touch, and the motor vehicles would warm the cockles of the present-day collector's heart. Scenes like this are a reminder that, in the depression years, many a large car was driven into a scrapyard in near-perfect condition, and that in those seemingly far-off days one could purchase a 'runner' for, almost literally, a bob or two.

# 8
# TRAFFIC & ACCIDENTS

The restrictions of 1914–18 naturally reduced greatly the number of motor vehicles in use in Britain, and in fact it was not until 1920 that the number of private cars and the number of motor vehicles of all sorts exceeded the previous highest total. By the census of 1925, the total of all motor vehicles in Britain topped the million mark for the first time, out of which total private cars accounted for 695,634. By 1931, however, the total of private cars alone had exceeded the million mark with a figure of 1,103,715, according to figures published by the Society of Motor Manufacturers and Traders. In the same year, 1931, the same body also published figures of accidents attributed to road vehicles of all kinds, and for all classes of road vehicles the number of fatal accidents was said to be 5,746 and non-fatal accidents 129,756 for the year. Out of these totals, private cars were said to have contributed 1,813 and 48,307 respectively – figures which, in the light of the many fewer vehicles then than today and the lower average speeds of the time, are grisly reminders of the toll of death and injury that an increasing subservience to the motor vehicle brought with it.

These figures do throw into perspective the widely believed and nostalgic notion that in the inter-war period the roads were blissfully open and free, just as they highlight the salient difference between motoring, in general terms, in the 1920s and '30s, as compared with the pre-1914 era. The inter-war years made plain the need for increasing control over the ever-increasing volume of traffic. It was not until the late 1920s that roads designed, not adapted, as motor roads came into being, something that gained momentum until 1939. The majority of roads were still, of course, those that had served the pre-motor age, modified only in respect of surface and detail; such roads still form a great part of Britain's road mileage today, when their inadequacy is ever more apparent.

Whether or not the motorcar is worth the enormous cost, both in financial and environmental terms, is outside the scope of these remarks; the fact remains that the new arterial roads and by-passes of the 1930s were mostly far uglier than today's motorways, and it was in those same years that the increasing volume of motor traffic began to be a real threat to many aspects of the social environment.

One looks at the photographs of the period and reads into them only too readily an impression of, in traffic terms, uncrowded and unfettered spaciousness compared with what we know today; the figures quoted show the other side of the coin.

This 1923 Aston Martin, at one time owned by the author, suffered a serious crash when its first owner, Capt. J. C. Douglas, impaled it on a road bollard in London.

*Opposite:* Before and after... This Riley Redwing has suffered a nasty thump on the nose, but in the days before unitary construction, only the worst crunches were incapable of repair, and skilled labour was plentiful and cheap. It is a pity the photographer did not wait for the screen and spare tyre before recording the mechanic's handiwork. (*Watson's Motor Works*)

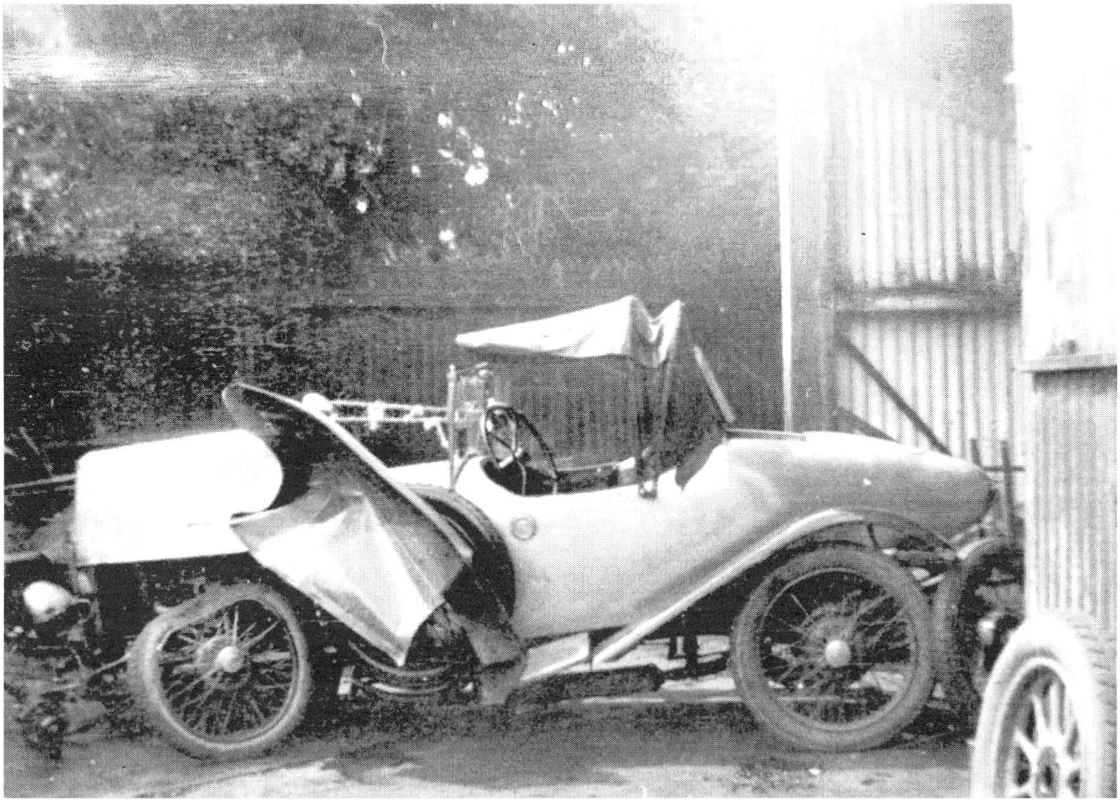

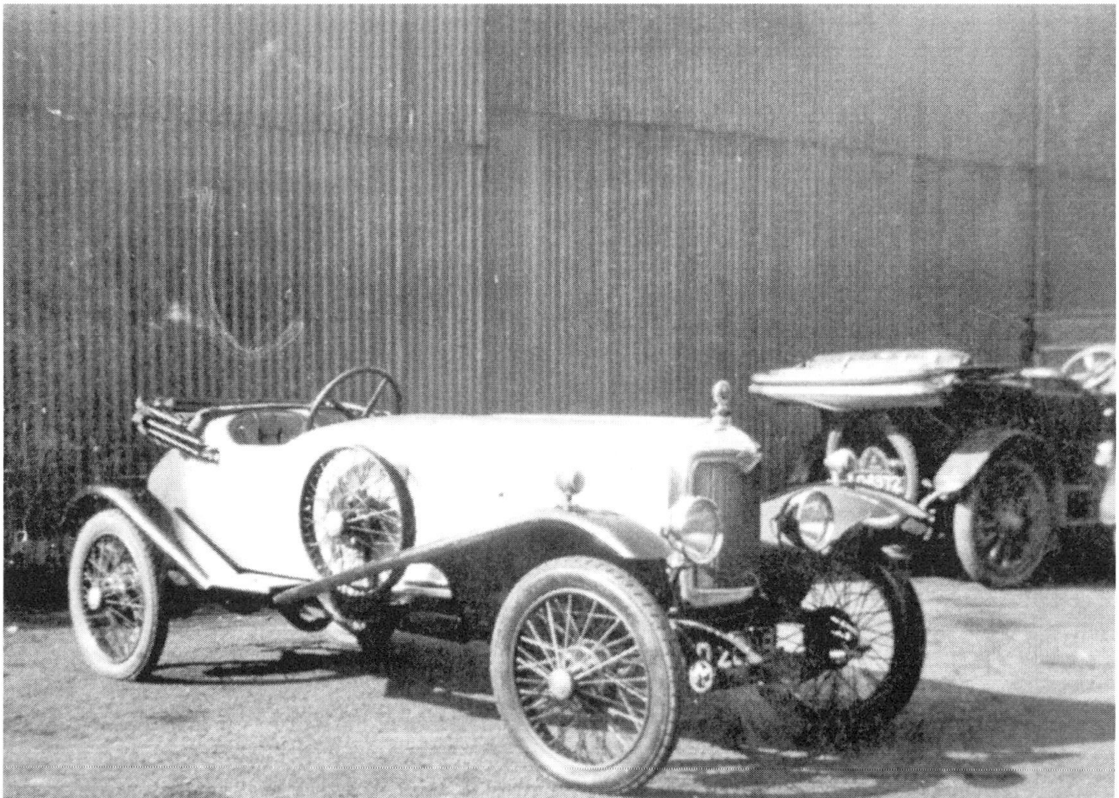

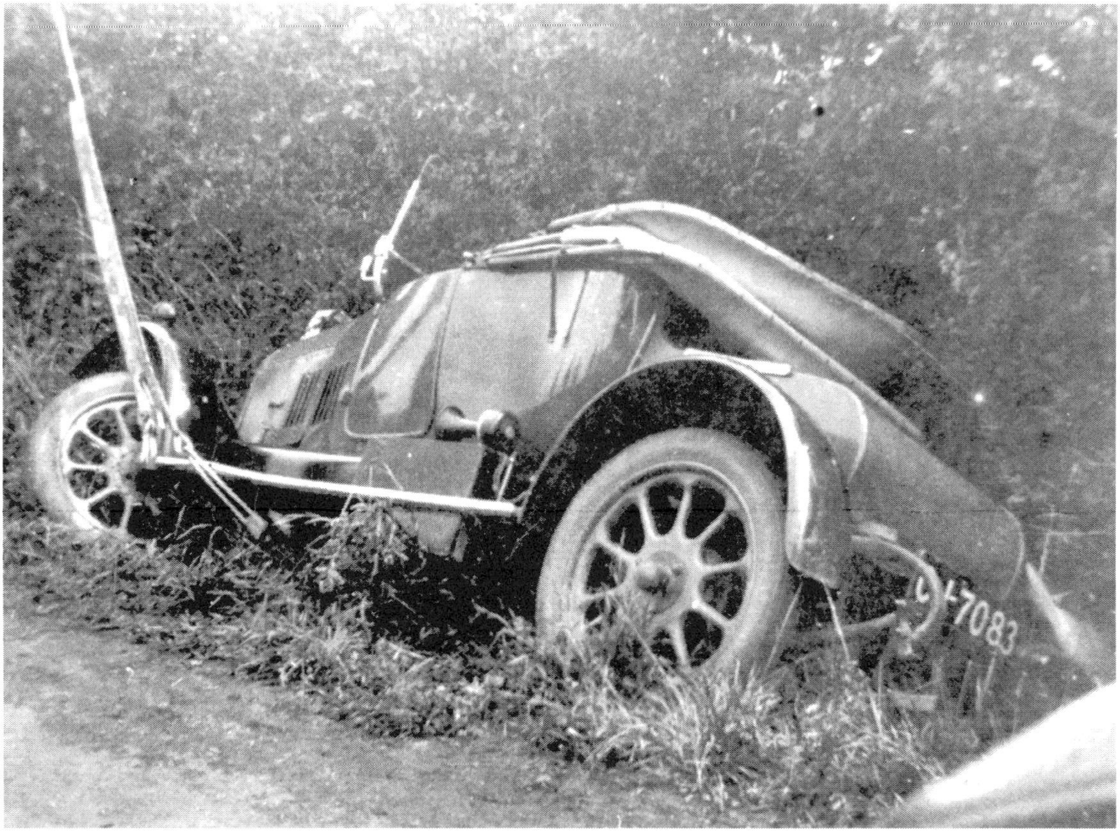

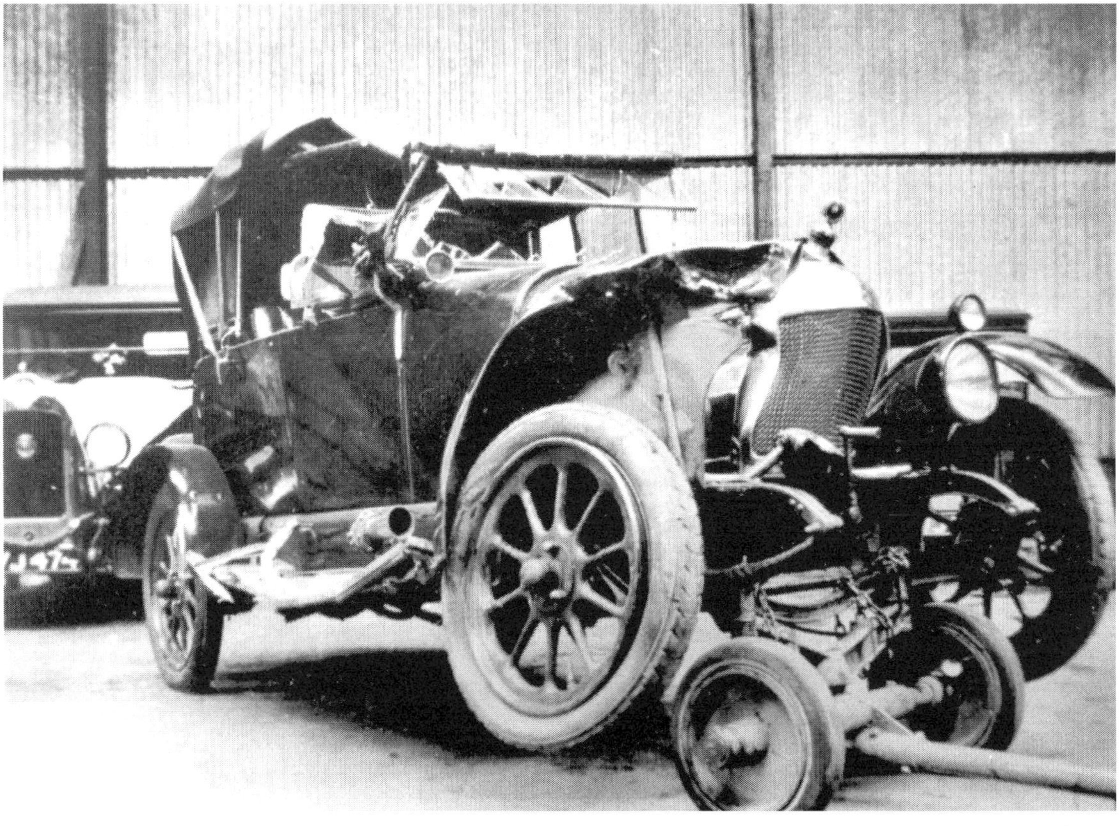

The main street in a county town in the late 1920s. Although the tracks of the former tramway system are still evident, the trams themselves have been withdrawn, thus easing the congestion previously inevitable. Within a year or so, the tracks too would have vanished. (*M. Dowty*)

*Opposite above:* This Herefordshire-registered 'Bullnose' Morris two-seater has met with a roadside mishap. The damage doesn't seem too serious and will doubtless be repaired when the car is taken to the local garage. (*F. Williams*)

*Opposite below:* Much less fortunate was this 'Bullnose' Morris, brought in on the good old towing ambulance that one still occasionally sees rusting and abandoned in country garages. The dire effects of broken windscreens in the days before safety glass became compulsory can be seen in this picture, and give point to the frequent advertisements in the press of the time advocating its use. (*F. Williams*)

Only in recent times have conservationists revolted against the mass of ugly street furniture that mass motoring brought with it, and which did so much to mar our townscapes. Here is a reminder – a street without these disfigurements, and without even a prowling traffic warden. Examples of Alvis, Austin, Jowett, Morris, Standard and Vauxhall cars may be seen.

The driver and a helper return this Austin 7 to an even keel after some over-enthusiastic cornering at Donington Park.

*Above and below:* The air of spaciousness and lack of congestion in each of these two views of provincial towns in the 1932–38 period is accentuated by the lack of road markings or signs; parking is easy and free and there is no obstruction to moving traffic. How much the motorist of today has lost!

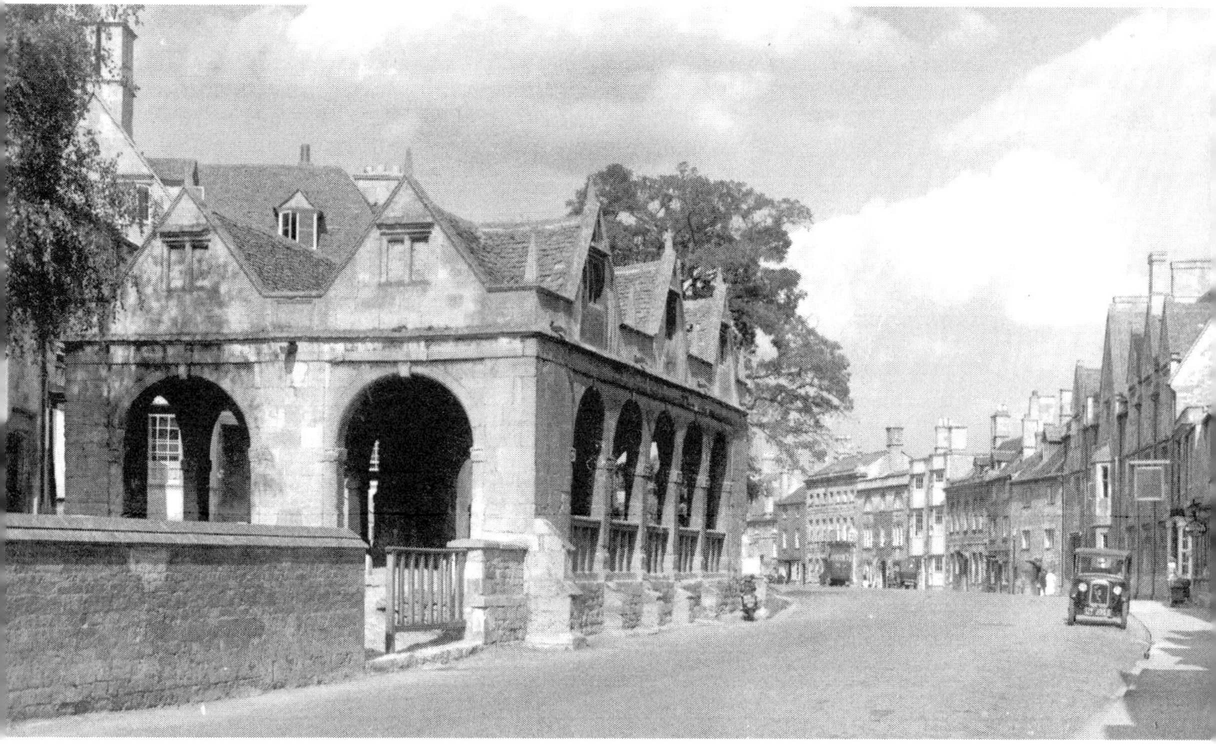

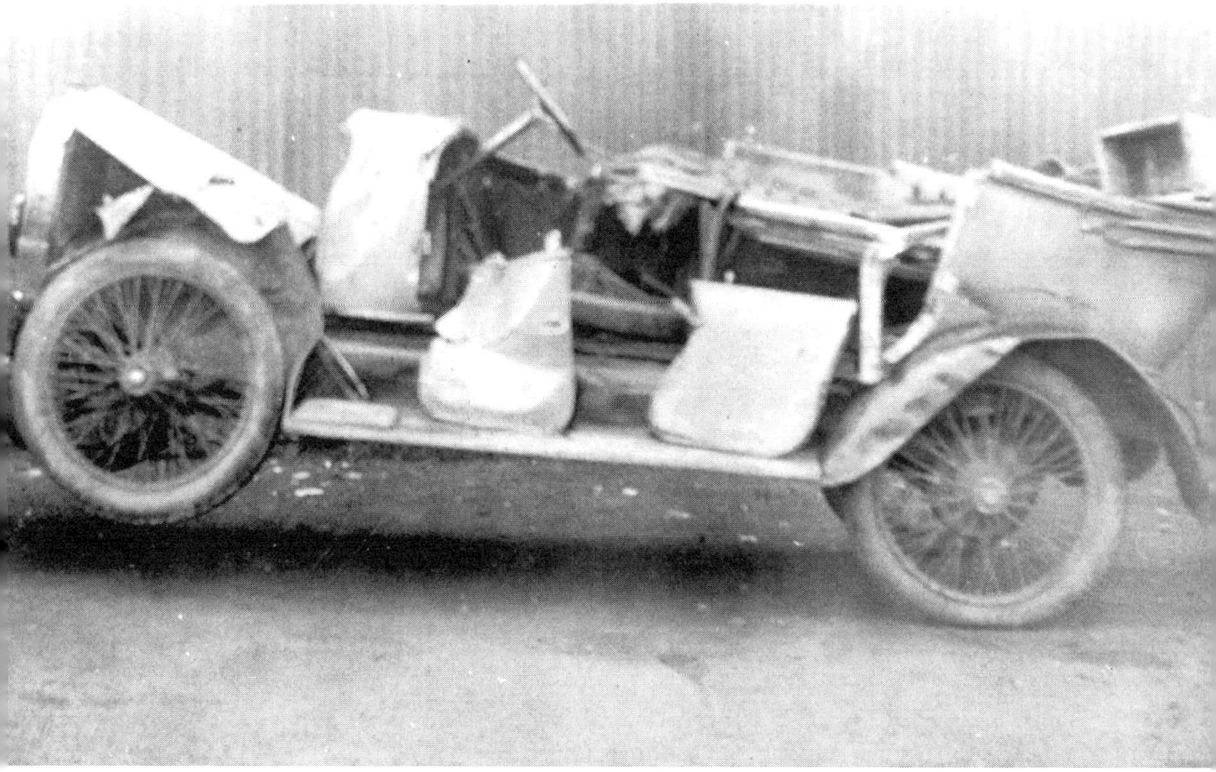

Traffic held up in Parliament Square, London, in the summer of 1932. The splendid 3-litre Bentley in the foreground (then by no means a new car) seems slightly aloof and straining for the open road. Could this be Lord Peter Wimsey, off to a case?

*Opposite above:* Today, few would credit that the attractive Cotswold town of Chipping Campden once had such peaceful streets.

*Opposite below:* This Vauxhall tourer seems to have made a determined attempt at destroying itself. It is probably too badly damaged to repair. (*Watson's Motor Works*)

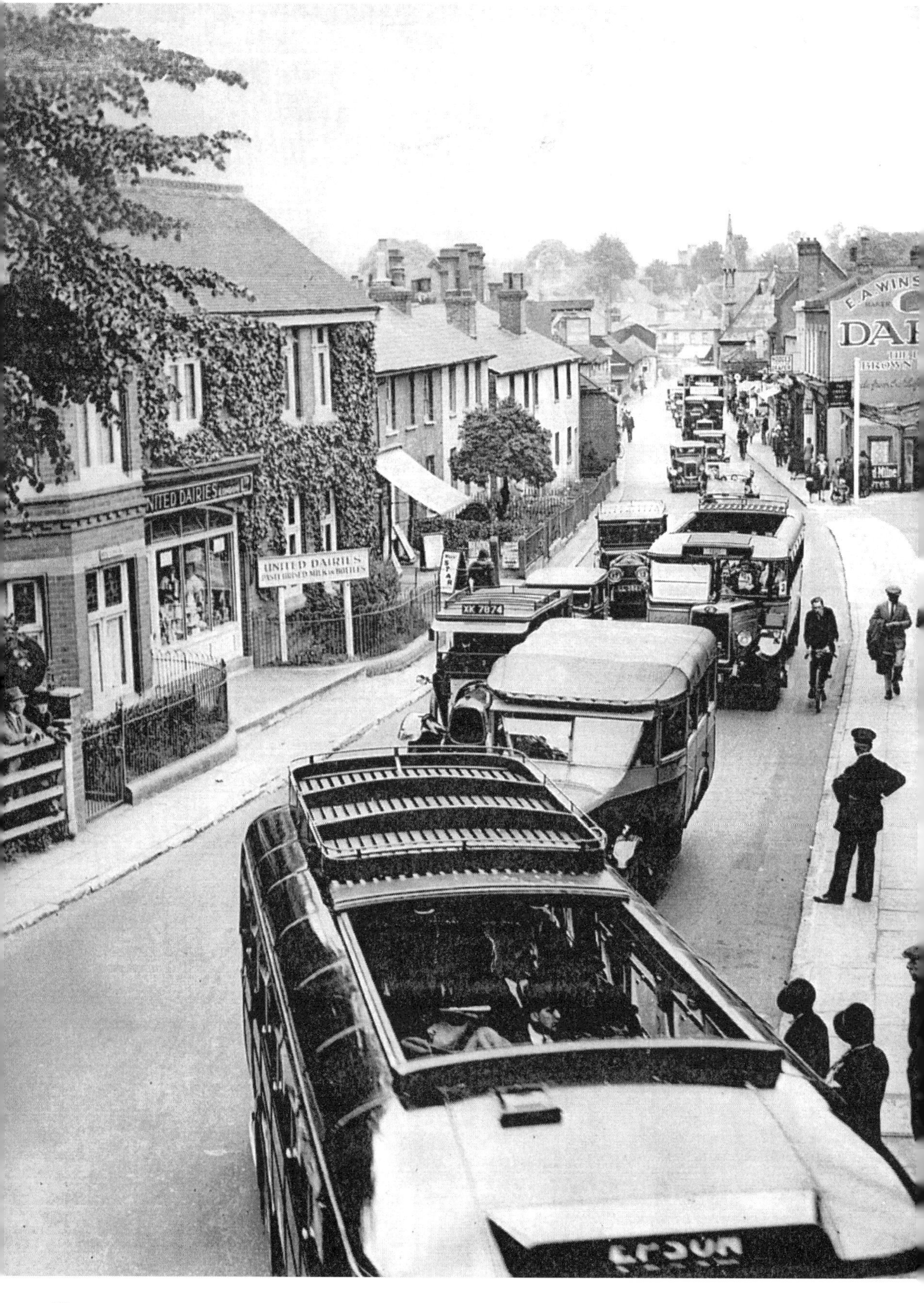
UNITED DAIRIES
PASTEURISED MILK in BOTTLES
XK 7874

It looks like a peaceful rural scene, but look closely and you will see that this Morris Eight tourer of the mid-1930s has wartime headlamp masks.

*Opposite:* Traffic en route to the Derby passes through Ewell West, Surrey, on Derby Day, 1931. The procession reveals a splendid variety of vehicles.

By 1939, war was to wreak six years of havoc. Here a Flying Standard 9 with a Worcester mark (FK) provides a vehicle for the young member of the Home Guard – of *Dad's Army* fame.

# ABOUT THE AUTHOR

Formerly senior master and counter-tenor lay clerk at a Worcestershire choir school, A. B. Demaus's interests range from classical music to veteran and vintage motorcars and cycles. He has been the owner and user of many early cars and cycles over the years, and has his own collection of machines.

A. B. Demaus has contributed to all the leading journals in the field. Also available from Amberley Publishing is the Demaus-edited *Letters from HMS Britannia: William Lambert and the Late Victorian Navy*, a collection of letters describing W. S. Lambert's career patrolling the frontiers of the British Empire in the late nineteenth century.

ALSO AVAILABLE FROM AMBERLEY PUBLISHING

Jowett: A Century of Memories
Noel Stokoe

In 1906, brothers Benjamin and William Jowett designed and built their first car. Noel Stokoe brings together a potted history of the marque with a selection of letters from previous owners as well as many previously-unpublished images of Jowetts, using the archives of the Jowett Car Club, one of the oldest one-marque car clubs in existence.

978 1 4456 0087 1
176 pages, 80 b&w and 30 colour illustrations

Available from all good bookshops or order direct
from our website www.amberleybooks.com

ALSO AVAILABLE FROM AMBERLEY PUBLISHING

Motoring Around Kent
Tim Harding & Bryan Goodman

Covering the period up to and including the Second World War, the early years of Kentish motoring are told through a superb collection of images.

978 1 84868 575 8
160 pages, 200 b&w images

Available from all good bookshops or order direct from our website www.amberleybooks.com

ALSO AVAILABLE FROM AMBERLEY PUBLISHING

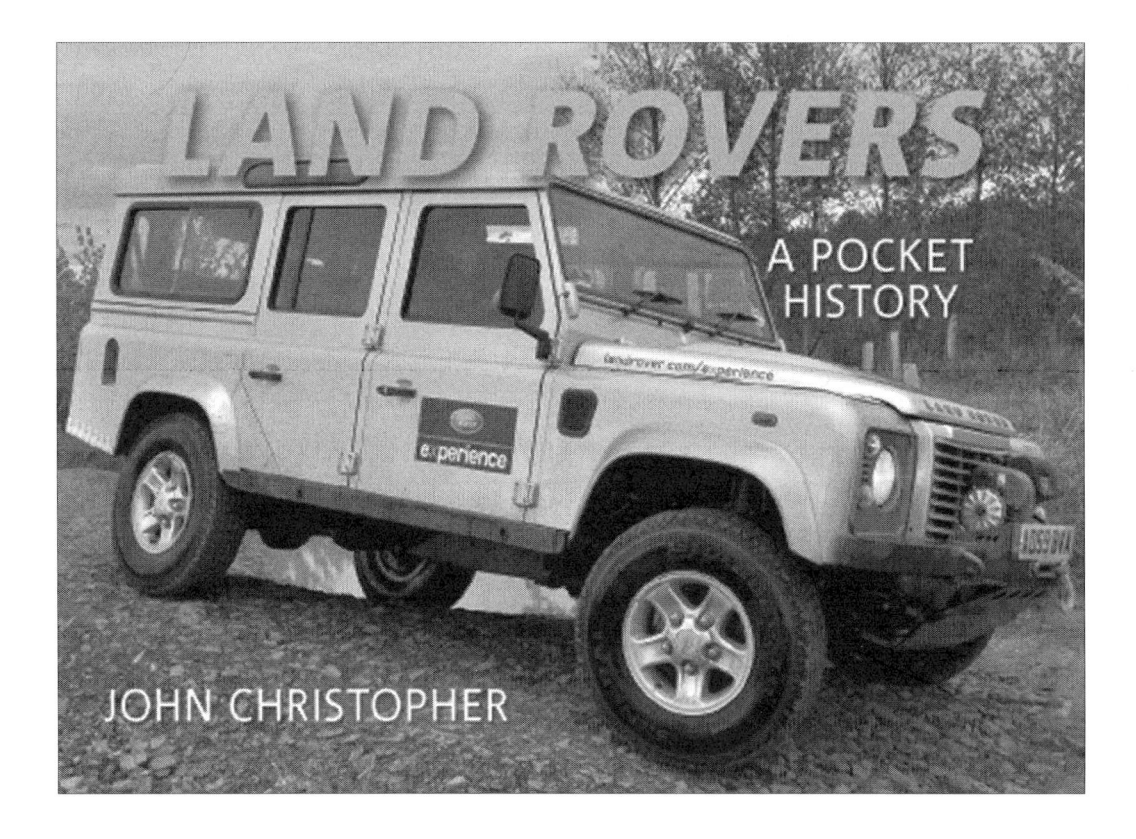

## Land Rovers: A Pocket History
John Christopher

In 1948, on the Isle of Anglesey, the first prototype Land Rover was put through its paces. It was a utilitarian four wheel-drive vehicle, designed for farmers, who could use it for a multitude of purposes. The vehicle, made to be simple and rugged, had an aluminium alloy body with a steel chassis. Intended as a simple stopgap for Rover, while post-war car production restarted, the Land Rover has proved to be an enduring British icon, advertised as the 'best 4x4 x far'.

*Land Rovers: A Pocket History* is profusely illustrated, detailed look at this British icon

978 1 84868 972 5
128 pages, 115 colour illustrations

Available from all good bookshops or order direct from our website www.amberleybooks.com